DR. MORGAN CUTLIP

*HOW COUPLES CAN TACKLE THE MENTAL LOAD FOR MORE FUN, LESS RESENTMENT, AND GREAT SEX

a better share

NELSON
BOOKS

An Imprint of Thomas Nelson

Published in Nashville, Tennessee, by Nelson Books, an imprint of Thomas Nelson. Nelson Books and Thomas Nelson are registered trademarks of HarperCollins Christian Publishing, Inc.

The author is represented by Alive Literary Agency, www.aliveliterary.com.

Thomas Nelson titles may be purchased in bulk for educational, business, fundraising, or sales promotional use. For information, please email SpecialMarkets@ThomasNelson.com.

Names and identifying characteristics of some individuals have been changed to preserve their privacy.

This book contains discussions of mental health topics, including anxiety, depression, and other related issues. The content is intended for informational purposes only and should not be considered a substitute for professional mental health advice, diagnosis, or treatment. If you are experiencing mental health challenges, please seek the help of a qualified healthcare provider.

Library of Congress Cataloging-in-Publication Data

Names: Cutlip, Morgan, 1982- author.
Title: A better share : how couples can tackle the mental load for more fun, less resentment, and great sex / Morgan Cutlip.
Description: Nashville, Tennessee : Nelson Books, 2025. | Includes bibliographical references. | Summary: "Relationship expert Dr. Morgan Cutlip helps couples view the mental load—the endless and mostly invisible work of managing a household and family—as a shared enemy to conquer versus a problem they have with each other, offering practical solutions for navigating the most common pain points couples struggle with"— Provided by publisher.
Identifiers: LCCN 2024048903 (print) | LCCN 2024048904 (ebook) | ISBN 9781400239672 (hardcover) | ISBN 9781400239689 (ebook)
Subjects: LCSH: Communication in marriage. | Man-woman relationships. | Sexual division of labor. | Housekeeping.
Classification: LCC HQ734 .C967 2025 (print) | LCC HQ734 (ebook) | DDC 646.7/82—dc23/eng/20241211
LC record available at https://lccn.loc.gov/2024048903
LC ebook record available at https://lccn.loc.gov/2024048904

Printed in the United States of America

25 26 27 28 29 LBC 5 4 3 2 1

TO MY FIRST AND FOREVER
LOVE, CHAD. THANK YOU
FOR BEING THE BEST
TEAMMATE AND A HUSBAND
THAT CONTINUES TO GROW
WITH ME. I AM SO BLESSED
TO CALL YOU MINE.

CONTENTS

Part 3: Practically Speaking

CHAPTER
1

fully loaded

I woke up at 3 a.m. with the nagging feeling that Chad hadn't really gotten the message that he was in charge of the balloons for Roy's birthday party. A few days before, as I was rushing around the house—overwhelmed, flustered, and likely a little bit scary—Chad had asked me, as he regularly did, if there was anything that I needed him to take care of.

I realize that this question alone may trigger you—believe me, I was also triggered. I responded, "Balloons, just handle the balloons. Start to finish. I want the number eight, baseballs, and a cluster of primary colors. There's a local place that even delivers."

"I'm on it," he replied, and that was the end of it.

And now here I was, restless and worried a few days later, wondering, *Is he really on it? Are the balloons really handled?* To give the full context, I wasn't obsessing over the balloons or having high balloon standards; it's just that they were a line on my mental checklist that I thought had been ticked off, yet I wasn't absolutely certain. I wanted this out of my head and off my list because I had other stuff to get on with, like ordering the food for the birthday party, making sure the gift bags were made up, wrapping Roy's presents, confirming the location of the party with our guests, picking up plates and napkins, grabbing

1

crap to stuff in the piñatas, washing Roy's baseball uniform, finishing up Christmas shopping, finding a recipe for my mom's birthday cake, prepping the house for my in-laws, washing clothes for an upcoming family trip, making sure the kids had shoes that fit and weren't covered in mud, making dog food, giving the dog a bath. And this didn't even include any of my work obligations. I could go on but this book isn't going to be that long . . . You get the idea.

The balloons were a minor task on my list among a slew of other tasks that were whizzing around my brain at three in the morning. I wanted to free up the teeny bit of space that handing off these balloons would offer. Sort of like having a sip of water when you're dying of thirst in the desert. It doesn't totally satisfy, but it offers a blip of relief.

I spent the next hour marinating in my own panic. You may know this place: Your thoughts are spinning, you're doing advanced calculations trying to figure out when you're going to do what and how to maximize output and minimize effort—and then it hits you that you're not actually sleeping and are going to be totally spent the next day. And everything is going to feel harder. And suddenly you have an entirely new topic to worry about, taking you deeper into your sleepless night self-sabotage.

Eventually, I dozed off, and when I woke at 6 a.m., I walked upstairs where Chad, when he's not traveling for work, is usually perched on the couch early in the morning doing work on his computer and drinking coffee. As I approached, I was acutely aware that I had an intensity about me. I didn't mean to; it's just that the holiday season, which also happens to be jam-packed with birthdays in our family, had increased my stress so immensely that I felt like a revved engine. Someone or something had its foot on the gas and I was trying to appear chill, when inside I was anything but.

"Hey, babe. Do you have a second to chat about Roy's birthday?" I asked.

"Sure," Chad said as he looked up from his computer.

"So, I was up last night a little overwhelmed about all I've got to do for his party, and for some reason, I have this worry that you didn't fully get that you're in charge of the balloons."

Chad responded with "Just tell me when and where to pick them up."

I don't fully remember my reaction because it was like the blue screen of death that appears on a computer—I just malfunctioned. Things went blank. I was angry and irritated and also disappointingly impressed by my intuition. Somehow I knew that he hadn't really gotten it. Still, I couldn't believe it.

"I asked you to handle them start to finish," I replied.

The conversation unfolded for us in a way that I bet is familiar to you. I came in a bit hot when expressing my irritation:

M: *"Chad, I thought you had this and you don't."*

C: *"You didn't communicate it clearly. You know I live by my calendar. It wasn't on there, so it doesn't exist."*

M: *"It's not my fault you didn't put it on the calendar. Do you expect me to double-check if you put things on the calendar? I don't want to hold this in my mind. I wanted you to handle it."*

C: *"Well, I don't know what type of balloons you want, what your vision is, or how many balloons are in a cluster."*

M: *"You manage tons of employees. Just figure it out. I don't care."*

C: *"Well, I don't want to get it wrong."*

We went round and round and this whole balloon debacle got blown way out of proportion (pun intended). This situation seemed simple on the surface. I had asked for the balloons to be taken care of. He agreed. End of story. But most relationship interactions are more fully loaded than they appear. In truth, Chad could have just owned it, apologized, and we would have moved on.

But we both had valid perspectives. I do have standards for our parties and what things look like, and I am the one who has always ordered the balloons. Asking Chad to take care of the balloons was an exception to our normal. And despite the fact that I tend to have somewhat high standards for our parties, I just didn't care about the balloons, yet he assumed I did. It makes sense he was unsure how to move forward; this task has always been mine, and I expected him to know what to do on his first try.

Yet my ask wasn't unreasonable. He could have figured it out, or he could have asked me to clarify.

When both sides of this story are really examined, Chad and I felt the situation was unfair. I wanted him to own it. He wanted more details. What we really needed was to find a better way to share this task. While the interaction is relatable on the surface, underneath there are much deeper forces at play. I wanted him to share my perspective better; he wanted the same. He wanted me to express expectations more clearly; I thought I had. I wanted him to take ownership; he missed that mark. We both needed to share accountability for what happened. This is the complicated aspect of the mental load: There are two perspectives and more complex dynamics at play than just divvying it up. What Chad and I needed was a plan for a better way to share.

The Mental Load

Welcome. I truly believe that if you resonate with any part of the story I just shared, you've come to the right book. My goal is to help you and your partner find a better share. Not only a better share of who does what around the home and in family life, but a better share in terms of how you and your partner are able to communicate around this typically touchy and triggering topic.

Part of finding greater ease in your relationship around the mental load is being able to regularly talk about it without it turning into a fight. When you're already exhausted from dealing with your everyday demands, you don't have the extra energy to trudge through an argument every time this topic comes up. This book offers more than a plan to renegotiate roles and responsibilities; it will prompt you to dig a little deeper, see things in your relationship in a new light, and ultimately come out the other side feeling like you and your partner are better off than you were before.

So why did I share that personal, and potentially discrediting, story about the balloons? Because there is something really important about relationships and the mental load that you must know as we get into this book. *The mental load and any issues you've experienced around it in your relationship do not exist compartmentalized in a box separate from everything else in your relationship. Your relationship is dynamic—if you upset one part of it, other parts will be affected.*

The reality that your relationship is dynamic can work in both the positive and the negative directions. When the mental load is handled in a way that feels unfair, or your partner minimizes the reality of it or gets defensive every time it comes up, over time your closeness and connection will start to deteriorate. You will start to feel unsafe in your relationship and with your partner, and this can lead to more hostile exchanges or more withdrawn behavior.

However, when the mental load is handled in a way that feels good to both partners and you can approach each other to talk about your relationship with ease, your relationship bonds will start to strengthen. You will feel like you're on the same team and connected. This leads to greater feelings of love, attraction, trust, commitment, reliability, and usually a way more exhilarating sex life.

Something I've noticed is that most solutions offered around the mental load suggest it is one partner's job to pick up more of the slack. While this may be part of the solution, it neglects consideration for individual differences in work schedules, life circumstances, skill sets, and nuance for how relationships realistically function. If the solution is simply for one partner to "step it up," it suggests that one partner is failing the other. This approach can lead to contentiousness in the relationship and permission for the put-out partner to be pissed off and petty. One of my intentions throughout this book is to offer perspectives to each partner that otherwise may never be expressed. Consider me your middle woman, bridging the gap between your two worlds and experiences, speaking directly to you without judgment or hostility but with the goal of helping you feel better about the mental load in your relationship *and* more connected as a couple.

Throughout these chapters you will see boxes that provide perspectives for each partner, most of which come from the data I collected and interviews I conducted. They are labeled "His Perspective" or "Her Perspective." In full transparency, I struggled with exactly how to identify these sections, but my expertise and research is with heterosexual couples. If you are not in a heterosexual relationship, this book may not be for you. I still believe that you will gain insights, but you may not relate to the language. However, I want to stay true to my experience and expertise and not make irresponsible generalizations.

Also, if you're in a relationship where the roles are reversed and you're a man who is carrying more of the mental load of the home and family, please know that the concepts will still apply if you can see beyond the language. Even though this may not be true in your family, the reason I wrote the book making the assumption that the woman is carrying the bulk of the mental load is because research continually shows this is the case. Writing a book with this much nuance and with endless variations of relationship situations is tricky, and I had to paint with broad brushstrokes. Yet, I know there is a great amount of overlap of experiences—my data and review of the research show that—and I believe that these sections will offer more benefit than harm.

Get A Load of These Three Things

I fully believe in informed consent, and I know that reading (or listening) to a book is an investment of time and time is finite. Feeling good about how you spend it is important, so I'm going to be direct and tell you three specific things I want you to be on board with as a reader. Then I'll tell you exactly what you can expect from the rest of this book.

1. **Your partner isn't the enemy.** Repeat after me: "My partner isn't the enemy." I mean it—say it out loud if you have to. This is

important. The enemy is our socialization and how that works against us. Specifically, how it sets women up to give their all to the point of being consumed by and lost in their relationships, ultimately burning out. And men are socialized to be highly sensitive to criticism and feelings of failure because they've been taught it's their job to rescue their partner and keep her happy and safe all while suppressing most emotions besides anger. The enemy is the busyness of Western society that expects us to hustle our butts off with little to no support for working families and mothers. The enemy is the expectation of constant hustle and productivity, which makes most of us feel hurried and as if we're spinning through life unable to actually rest because something always needs done. The enemy is social media and other information we consume that makes us feel like everyone has a better partner, house, vacation, kids, wardrobe, pantry, body, skincare routine, diet, and so on, keeping us always in lack mode versus feeling abundant in our enoughness. These are the true enemies. See them clearly for what they are and try to disengage from friendly fire.

I can already hear the objections to this: "Well, my partner is outright nasty—you're telling me they aren't the enemy?!" Okay, there is a caveat; remember there are always individual differences and exceptions to the rule. There are some partners who, no matter what you try, are resistant to growing and changing. These partners become a major part of the problem. However, some partners appear this way but then change when deeper issues are addressed, so be patient to see which camp your partner falls into. However, if you're in a relationship with a partner that exhibits any type of abuse (emotional, verbal, physical), this is a hard-line deal-breaker. Abuse should never be tolerated; your safety is the number one priority here.

2. **Leave your ego at the door.** I'm going to challenge you to embrace humility and ditch your ego. This is hard, but if you want to have a great relationship, it's necessary. The more you defend your stance, the more you will push your partner away.

The more you criticize and nitpick, the more distance you will create. If you can lean into humility (which is a sign of ego strength, by the way), you can accomplish some really wonderful things in your relationship that will take it to a level of closeness and connection you've not imagined or likely experienced. I am requesting that you approach this book with openness and a commitment to grow. If you want to win arguments in your relationship, by all means go for it, but I can guarantee that if *you* win, the relationship is losing.

3. **You have personal power.** If your partner changes nothing, when you make a change, the relationship will still shift. This is hard for some people to wrap their heads around because it's so much easier to point fingers and say, "Well, I'd be more pleasant if you'd help me out more," or "Well, I'd help out more if you'd actually act like you like me," or some iteration of these statements. One person can shift the whole relationship on their own because we each have personal power. I want to remind you of this because, ideally, both of you are reading this book together and are committed to finally resolving this relationship issue. However, I'm a realist and know that some partners won't as easily engage in this work. Either way, you will gain insights and practical tools throughout this book to help you shift your dynamic on your own. I want you to feel hopeful and encouraged by this. You have options. You have power. Hang in there.

Okay, now that you have those three things in mind, here's what you need to know as you navigate this book. The first part, "What Is the Mental Load and Why Is It Wreaking Havoc in Your Relationship?," is going to define and explain the mental load so it's simple and easy to grasp. One of the most common frustrations I hear from women is that their partner "just doesn't get it" when it comes to the mental load. This section will help with that. You will gain an understanding of why the mental load isn't a simple list of chores and how it differs from carrying a mental load at work. This section will also break down a common myth about sharing responsibilities in the home and family that leads to women not feeling like it's okay to ask for involvement from their partner. Finally, you will learn how to prepare your relationship for having difficult discussions about the mental load and learn some basic tools for navigating these conversations to prevent things from getting heated or know how to deal if it does.

The next part, "Sharing Is Caring," is going to cover four areas that—if you and your partner fully address and share—will help you not just master the mental load but dramatically transform your relationship:

1. Perspective
2. Expectations
3. Ownership
4. Accountability

I'll take you on a deep-ish dive and then bring you back to the surface and equip you with practical tools and strategies to deal with these challenges. These four areas are informed by research on the mental load and by the hundreds of respondents to my survey data and qualitative questions as well as over a dozen interviews with men and women about the mental load. You'll come away with a broadened perspective into each other's innermost workings and individual differences. Once you have perspective, you can capitalize on your individual differences and work as a team.

The final section of this book, "Practically Speaking," will outline action plans and talking points for three main things: an agenda for regularly talking about the mental load with your partner, how to reconnect sexually, and how to introduce the concept of the mental load to your kids. I am a huge believer that we can change society and our world by changing our relationships at home. It's a bottom-up approach, but it's powerful, plus it will offer you so much more sanity in your family life as you navigate the mental load for the modern family.

Now that you know what's ahead, let's do this!

PART
1

what is the

mental load,

and why is it

wreaking havoc in

your relationship?

CHAPTER
2

it's not you; it's the mental load

While the concept of the mental load has been discussed in various ways since the 1970s, the term "mental load" went viral in 2017 after a French artist named Emma Clit created a comic called "You Should've Asked,"[1] and then in 2019 Eve Rodsky addressed this pain point in her bestselling book *Fair Play*. Since then, millions of women have become familiarized with the term and what it means. Ultimately these women have breathed a huge sigh of relief at the fact that this experience of feeling overwhelmed and overloaded isn't unique to them, but rather is an almost universally shared experience of women, and specifically mothers. However, I dare you to go to your next work function and ask the dude sitting next to you about the mental load and watch him look at you like you've got lobsters crawling out of your ears. Women tend to know what it is; men tend to zone out at the mention of it or have no idea what we're talking about. The conversation tends to go the same way:

"Okay, so what is the mental load?"

"Oh, well, it's the mental running to-do list we, meaning usually women, carry around in our heads."

"Okay . . . so why don't you just make a list?" Or they shrug it off, like *What's the big deal? That's just life.* Men struggle to get it.

Maybe you've found yourself in a conversation with your partner about the mental load and you've struggled to get him to really understand what it is and why it's such a major deal in your relationship. I know I've sat across from my husband trying to articulate my mental load to him, just to feel ridiculous and silly as I listed the things out. One by one they don't seem that major. Each item seems doable and easily handled.

But here's the thing: While the mental load can sound like a list of minor things (thinking about what's for dinner, filling out forms for kids' schools, remembering registration dates for flag football), often one item can be unpacked like a tiny mental suitcase to contain multiple steps, which all take up vital energy. Energy that doesn't get poured into things like self-care, the relationship, getting in a sexy state of mind, and so on.

HER PERSPECTIVE

I feel like he thinks I'm inventing things to concern myself with. He diminishes my real concerns and stress over the mental load, which makes me feel gaslit and unappreciated.

My partner doesn't understand how much work goes into running a household and caring for our children. He downplays what I do and makes me feel small with his response when I share how I'm feeling, even if my delivery is positive.

Or maybe you've tried to have the conversation about it with your partner and it just went sideways. If this is you, please know you're not alone. I surveyed 536 women and here's what the most common responses were when I asked "When you try to talk about the mental load to your partner, what happens?"*

- 61 percent responded, "I'm told, 'Well, just tell me what to do.'"
- 53 percent said, "It just turns into a competition of who does what or who does more."
- 52 percent said, "My partner gets defensive."
- 48 percent said, "My partner just doesn't understand the concept of the mental load."
- 37 percent said, "My partner tells me to just not do so much."
- 19 percent said, "I have just given up."

Talking about the mental load is one of the trickiest terrains to navigate. Once you get this down, you and your partner will be better able to deal with the weight of it all and ultimately find a better way to share the burden. In order to have the conversation, let alone get good at it, you've got to be on the same page with understanding what the mental load is.

Defining the Mental Load

The broad definition is this: The mental load is the invisible running to-do list that you carry in your head. Steps involved in the mental load include anticipating needs, identifying options, deciding among the options, and then monitoring the results.[2] It consists of things like

- remembering what needs to be done and when;
- keeping track of the inventory of the home;
- delegating tasks, and monitoring and following up to make sure they get done;

---

* Survey participants were able to select all responses that felt applicable.

- researching, planning, and managing the social calendar of the family;
- helping the kids sort through conflicts and coming up with solutions; and
- reading the parenting books and being the one to initiate conversations when your relationship is needing attention.

The mental load is largely invisible, but you can think of it as having three distinct categories:

1. **The cognitive:** The tasks that require mental effort. If you work outside the home and have said, "I have a mental load, too, mine is just at work," likely this load is filled with cognitive tasks. These are the lists of things you have to do and remember, like responding to emails, thinking about what's for dinner, submitting payroll, remembering that you need to sign the permission slip for your daughter's field trip, and so on.
2. **The physical:** The stuff that is done for the family and home that requires physical effort—things like doing the laundry, washing the dishes, or mowing the lawn. It's usually the most visible part of the mental load, but it still requires that someone keep track of the tasks.
3. **The emotional:** This one is the kicker. It is the weight you carry managing the *experiences* of family members. It's the mapping out of potential causes and effects and what that means for the people you love. This is what's often missing from the mental load of the workplace.

For example, while thinking about what's for dinner is a cognitive aspect of the mental load and making dinner is the physical load, the emotional side may be factored in as well. It sounds like this: *Well, if I make chicken Parmesan, Noah won't eat the chicken because it's breaded and Mia won't eat the tomato sauce because it hurts her stomach. Okay, so I could make mac and cheese instead, but my husband doesn't like that. Hmm, what is a win for everyone?* Or *If we choose this school, Stella won't be with her friends anymore, and what will that do to her development? But the school has a better reputation. Will I be scarring her for life by ripping her away from her friends or stunting her educational development by not putting her in the better school?*

Furthermore, the emotional load is internal—and invisible—so it's always with you no matter if you're at work or at home. The emotional load is the reason why you may have not felt the intensity of the mental load before kids entered the picture. You still had the cognitive and physical, but the emotional piece was far less present, because you mostly worried about yourself and to some extent your partner. But kids—that's taking it up a notch.[*]

Managing the emotional side of the mental load is exhausting because it never ends, it causes anxiety and rumination, and it's

---

[*] You may have noticed that you or your partner have a lot more anxiety than you did before kids or that you (or your partner) seem to operate at a baseline of stressed out. This emotional piece is the likely culprit. And if you wonder why you work at a stressful job but your partner seems really stressed out in the home, or you work at a stressful job yet it feels like a break, this is probably the reason why. The emotional work is significant, it's strategic, and it feels like the stakes are very high.

incredibly hard to delegate to others or automate because it involves a deep knowledge of and love for your family that can't easily be replicated or handed off. And, for the most part, the bulk of the mental load (all three aspects) is carried by women. I realize this may cause some of you to bristle, but know this:

1. There are exceptions to everything. The way your home operates may look different, and this may not be true for you. In your home, your roles may be reversed or even more fluid. Please know that the concepts of this book will apply no matter who carries the bulk of the load.

2. While everyone has a mental load of some kind, this book is referring to the mental load of the home and family. For example, you may say, "I have a mental load with my job." I have absolutely no doubt that you do. I remember talking to a guy I was interviewing on our podcast and I asked him, "If you had a pie chart of your mental load, how much is devoted to work versus family and home stuff?" He responded, "Around 75 percent is devoted to work." Likely, this is how many men would respond; their primary mental load domain is work. However, when women work full-time, they still carry the bulk of the mental load at home. So this distribution of energy invested in each domain doesn't seem to translate in the same way for men and women, which is why the mental load at home still requires attention, otherwise feelings of unfairness and resentment will creep in.

Everyone carries a mental load. Even our kids. But one of the key differences is that the mental load of the family and home is not clearly owned by anyone until someone takes on the responsibility. This is where feelings of resentment can creep in. When she feels like "I didn't sign up for this," or "How did this become mine? We never even talked about it," that's when the mental load starts to be a problem.

Additionally, most of the mental load of the home is about caring for others. While the mental load of work can be stressful and intense, it's often about your personal performance or tasks, not necessarily intuiting the needs, wants, desires, and so on of others. Plus, you get paid to do it. The daily act of pouring into others without pay, usually without reciprocation of care ("I care for everyone else, but who cares for me?"), and often without acknowledgment, prestige, and appreciation starts to feel really unfair really fast. The emotional aspect is what takes the mental load to the next level because it's often tied in with the physical and cognitive aspects of the load. When these three are all required for a task, I call it the Triple Threat.

The Hunt for the Perfect Leggings

Our daughter, Effie, has a simple outfit formula: cardigan + T-shirt + leggings = happy place. However, her sensitivity to tags, fabric, and fit makes this simple formula hard to get right, especially the leggings part. If finding the perfect leggings were a valued talent, I'd be headlining in Vegas. Because the perfect fit didn't magically appear—not even close.

Her leggings tell a story of my mental load all on their own. They represent the management of frustration while struggling to decipher our daughter's discomfort (emotional); the sweat of my detective work to figure out which pair of pants met her criteria for the perfect fit and softness (cognitive, emotional); hours shopping online and in person to find styles she could try; trips to the post office to return my failed attempts; the incompletion of the task that hung out in my head, distracting me from other tasks like an open tab (cognitive, emotional); fitting yet another leggings hunt into my busy schedule; buying them; washing them; and folding them (physical).

Those leggings may just be my legacy. If I do nothing else with my life, at least I can say I found the right leggings. And since it was requested by one of the women I interviewed when writing this book, I've created a visual of the mental load. Ask and you shall receive! The visual of the leggings situation on the next page breaks down the three aspects of the mental load.

the mental load

physical
- Shopping online for leggings
- Going to the store to buy the leggings
- Going to the post office to return the leggings
- Having our daughter try them on
- Washing them
- Folding them and putting them away

cognitive
- Keeping track of leggings stock and what has holes
- Remembering what size our daughter wears at which stores
- Remembering to return things on time
- Racking my brain for alternative stores to shop for said leggings

THE TRIPLE THREAT

emotional
- Regulating my irritation when yet another pair "won't work" or "is itchy" or "is too tight"
- Regulating our daughter when she is irritated by the fit
- Figuring out what our daughter does and doesn't like, knowing the sensory preferences that she can't articulate
- Considering all of our daughter's sensory sensitivities when shopping for leggings
- Paying attention to when our daughter's clothes are getting worn out, which impacts her feeling good in them when she wears them (this happens fast when you wear the same thing every day)

And this is just one item in our home tucked away, hidden from view, in our daughter's drawer. I could do this for nearly every dang thing in our house. This unpacking of the invisible steps that lead to the manifestation of something physical—this is the mental load. The invisibility of the steps is why partners fail to see it. The effort to explain all the steps is why most women don't even bother trying. And the behavior of "just handling it" is fueled by an often very real worry of "If I don't do it, who will?"

HIS PERSPECTIVE

I am really good at the doing, but the "seeing" is hard for me. I try but I struggle to see the invisible.

Most items women carry are Triple Threat items; therefore, they occupy a ton of space in their brain. Now, I realize it's just leggings, not the codes to nuclear bombs, but this seemingly minor stuff adds up. Yet the minor aspect of it can be why the mental load is so often minimized by partners and why they often end up invalidating their partner's overwhelm with "Who cares" or "It's no big deal" or "You're making this harder than you need to." But it's important to see how one simple thing unpacks to contain a ton of thought, physical exertion, and emotional energy. Not to mention the amount of time that was devoted to one singular item in the home—we're talking at least ten hours. Now multiply this out, and it explodes rather quickly.

Why the Mental Load Sucks the Life out of You

The mental load is almost always first felt and then later defined; it's visceral. For me, I'll experience a full mental load as a spinning sensation and tightness in my chest. I'm sure you have your own "at capacity" mental load symptoms. Maybe you forget things, feel hurried, or feel just plain overwhelmed. There are reasons why the mental load can suck the life out of you. Please know that it doesn't have to always be this way, but I do want to add some definition and explanation as to why this is so that you can call it out when you notice it happening in your life.

1. The mental load is invisible and takes up cognitive real estate.

In 1988 educational psychologist John Sweller articulated his theory on cognitive load, which basically said that our brains can only process and store a limited amount of information. Sweller estimated that at any given time we can hold around five to nine things in our working memory. When our brain tries to take in more information or more complex information all at once, it becomes cognitively overloaded. The result of a cognitively overloaded state is that it becomes difficult to think clearly, make sound decisions, and solve problems. You may think that holding only five to nine items in your working memory at once sounds laughable, but I'm willing to bet your mind is as jam-packed as my son's stuffy-filled bed. So, if you feel like you drop balls, are regularly forgetting things, or are just overall mentally fatigued, this is why.

Now let's couple this theory with another popular psychological theory on willpower—or, if you prefer, we can call it *ego depletion*. I'm going to give you the thirty-thousand-foot overview of this theory originally proposed by Roy Baumeister in 1998. This theory states that each person has a limited ability to exercise self-control (willpower) each day that gets used up by various normal tasks like making decisions, delaying gratification, controlling emotions, planning anything, exercising patience, and so on. Oh, and side note for all you parents: If you start the day on a crap night of sleep, you're beginning the day with less willpower available. If you go all day without really doing much to replenish your willpower and you have engaged in things that deplete it, you're likely going to finish the day a little on edge—or maybe even a lot on edge.

What this means for your state of mind is that the mental load likely maxes out your cognitive load, which means that you, your partner, or both of you are walking around mentally fatigued. This overload drains your willpower. Now toss in other willpower drains associated with the mental load—like planning and making decision after decision, plus tons of other normal life drains like exercising patience and not losing it emotionally—and now it makes total sense why you or your partner is completely maxed out. It should also make sense why you or your partner may be twirling around like a stress tornado, a little grumpier, or a little more on edge. Your ability to regulate your emotional state is impaired because you're mentally drained and your self-control is waning. And on top of all that, this is happening internally and is therefore invisible to your partner unless you explicitly spell it out for them.

HER PERSPECTIVE

It feels like a thorn. It's always there. I'm always thinking about it; it's part of my daily checklist. It's a constant "white noise" part of my daily routine that I wish was nonexistent.

> The mental load fully drains my tank, which means in turn
> I'm not able to be fully present or fully give in my relationship
> with my husband.

2. The mental load is mostly treadmill tasks vs. one-and-done.

One of my favorite things to share on my stories on Instagram is dinner ideas. In fact, I have a free resource with over thirteen pages of dinner ideas because coming up with dinner ideas is something I find incredibly draining. I mean, do we really need to eat every day? The summer is even more intense: three meals a day for at least three people, maybe four if Chad is around. It never ends. In the summer or on any school break, I feel like I'm a short-order cook, held captive in a kitchen that is never clean and always missing one ingredient. Cooking meals, especially cooking dinner, nearly every day is just one of the many treadmill tasks that make up part of the mental load. By this I mean it just never ends. There is no finish line. Actually, death. Death is the finish line. The bad news is you're dead. The good news is you don't have to decide what to make for dinner.

The mental load, especially for women, is typically composed of treadmill tasks. For example, cooking, shopping for food, doing laundry, stocking the toilet paper, keeping up to date on kids having shoes that fit, cleaning the toilets, vacuuming, and tidying up. Treadmill tasks keep on repeating, unlike the one-and-done tasks that occur less frequently and offer the feeling of satisfaction when they've reached a point of completion.

HER PERSPECTIVE

I feel like I'm on a hamster wheel that I can't get off. It's frustrating and exhausting.

I can't relax, I can't let go. I don't have fun, even in recreational situations. I can't relax because I know when

I get home I have to make dinner, do the laundry from whatever activity we were just doing, make sure the kids do their homework, etc.

I feel like I'm constantly on the go and have to be on point. There isn't any downtime to just sit and relax. It's always thinking about what's next and what needs to be done.

I have a husband who crushes it getting things done around the house. He can barely sit still and hates the idea of watching other people exercise, which means I don't lose him for hours at a time watching sports—he is so stinking handy it's bananas. In fact, he's so handy, I feel like I need to learn how to churn butter or some sort of old-timey skill that would be useful if we ever needed to live off the land or something. Anyway, his get-it-done ability enriches my life in more ways than I can count—but, in full transparency, there have been times that I've been insanely jealous about his contributions around the home.

Let me give you an example. We recently spruced up our backyard and he had this vision of building an outdoor kitchen-shed structure with a metal garage door and cabinets. It's really gorgeous—it could be on Pinterest or Houzz. Now, my husband is a busy guy. He travels a ton for his job and works incredibly hard for our family, but weekends at home are precious. They're precious for me . . . who needs a minute since I've been holding down the fort. They're precious for the kids because they miss him like crazy, and they're precious to Chad because he works long hours away from home.

But since he had this vision for our backyard paradise, he was hell-bent on building the structure. He's the type of guy who hates unfinished projects and he doesn't leave loose ends. But this endeavor was a bit more labor intensive than other projects he's taken on, so it would take several weeks. But at eight months it was still going strong. Now, let me be clear: I love it. It is a showstopper. It elevates our back-yard. But, every time he worked on it, it took away from any regular stuff that needed to be done in the home, and it put more on me to take care of the kids. Truthfully, I didn't mind this much. I knew he would much rather be hanging with us than working away outside. But here's the thing: When the kitchen was done, it was done. No going back to build it all over again. My husband is able to walk outside, hands on his hips, show it off when guests come over, and soak in all their praise. Unlike laundry. No one comes over and comments on how beautiful laundry looks folded up in our drawers. With the kitchen, there is a visible symbol of a project complete and very well done. The human spirit loves this; it needs this; it's good for the soul. While this project is an outlier, taking more than eight months, it is still a one-and-done job.

HIS PERSPECTIVE

I've realized I can really turn off worrying about stuff in the mental load, where it seems like she can't.

I really wish she would be easier on herself.

I definitely compartmentalize it differently than she does. I can turn it off, but it doesn't seem like she can.

One-and-done jobs offer a sense of satisfaction when they're complete. They don't feel as draining because there is a light at the end of the tunnel that promises a stopping point. Many of the treadmill tasks of the mental load fall to women (not all but most), and many of the one-and-done tasks fall to the men. This differential is important to note because when there is no end point to a task, there is no reprieve from it. It almost permeates every aspect of life. Sitting on the couch watching a movie: "Oh crap, I need to change over the laundry." Sitting in a meeting at work: "Oh shoot, I'm missing that one ingredient for dinner tonight." These whiplash interruptions to daily life create a sense of never being finished, never getting a break, and always having to be productive that so many women struggle with. These tasks never really seem to end—just ask a mother whose children are grown if they still worry about them. I guarantee they'll say a resounding yes.

The mental load is not just a simple list of things you or your partner has to do. It is the emotional labor that goes into caring for children and a family that never really ends, the invisible tasks that are magically completed that don't often get acknowledged, and it's the clutter in your mind that occupies precious real estate that could be devoted to more enjoyable and pleasurable activities. And it's predominantly carried by women whether or not they are stay-at-home moms, work part-time, or work full-time.

Now that you fully understand what the mental load is, I'll spend the next chapter explaining the two truths we need to accept about the mental load, and the lie we need to stop believing.

get a load of this

Recap for the partner who carries the mental load at home

If you feel like you're running on a hamster wheel, constantly going from task to task but never really moving forward, it's probably the mental load wearing you down. I hope defining this for you has allowed you to take a giant exhale. There's nothing wrong with you.

Load up on self-compassion and understanding. First, I want you to work on encouraging yourself with your words. The mental load is heavy; it makes sense that you feel burdened. Please stop beating yourself up about it and just take a moment to acknowledge that it is normal to feel the weight of it all.

Recap for the partner who carries less of the mental load at home

If your relationship feels like it's changed over the years and especially since having kids, it's likely in part due to the increase in the mental load for your partner. This doesn't necessarily mean you're failing or doing anything wrong, so try to ditch the defensiveness, and know that gaining a good understanding of the mental load will improve your relationship dramatically. Invest in this process and watch your relationship come back to life.

Also, none of this suggests you don't have a mental load of your own—everyone does. But remember that hers is likely centered on caring for others without much acknowledgment or appreciation and it likely came unexpectedly. You probably knew what you were getting into with your work mental load, but her home mental load, where the tasks and who takes them on are less clearly defined, may have come as a surprise. This can easily lead to the feeling of "Hey, why am I doing all this?"

Load up on empathy and understanding. We will talk more about how to work through the trouble spots with the mental load. But the more you can soften to her as she expresses overwhelm while also expressing some level of understanding, the more she will feel connected and close to you.

CHAPTER
3

two truths and a lie about the mental load

My husband, Chad, took a job that required travel in our fourth year of marriage. At the time, we didn't have any kids. I truly think there should be a term for marriage after kids, just like how kids' maturing is marked by the label *adolescence* or as women become mothers it's labeled *matrescence*. I think marriages need a term for this. Maybe "holdontoyourpantalones-escence" or something like that. Because marriage before kids is wildly different from marriage after kids. It isn't bad necessarily; in fact, it can bring depth and meaning and unimaginable love to our lives. But changes in life like traveling for work, moving, renovating a home, or taking a new job, which are usually exciting adventures before kids, become stressful endeavors after kids.

We went into our decision with guns-a-blazing, packin' a whole lot of excitement about Chad's potential for advancement in his company and fully armed with naivete. Yes, this job did launch Chad's career, but it also set us on a path filled with jobs that regularly required travel. This didn't matter too much . . . until we had our daughter, Effie.

I shared my story of my turbulent transition into motherhood in my first book, but this entrance into parenthood was also tricky for our marriage. Like most couples, we didn't do a great job talking about how we were going to divide up responsibilities after we had kids. It wasn't an issue for us before kids, so we didn't see it coming. Looking back, this was a major miscalculation on our part. We went from worrying only about ourselves to having a creature to feed, swing, swoosh, swaddle, change, bathe, entertain, carry, calm, and so on—overnight! The responsibilities piled on and we were buried. Well, actually, *I* was buried, because Chad was traveling. Which was then promptly followed by a relocation from Florida to California when Effie was around two months old.

I tell you all this because when I learned the term *mental load*, it was like the world came up and gave me a giant hug. Finally, a label for the dizzying overwhelm I experienced on a daily basis. However, when the term started to become more mainstream and more books and resources became available, I continued to run into the same snafu: I had a partner who was sometimes available and sometimes completely out of pocket. He often just wasn't around.

When I read things about how to divide up the load, it didn't work for us. I mean, it could for a day or two, but otherwise, it just didn't account for two truths that I think are really important to understand about the mental load before you try to tackle it.

Truth 1: The mental load is never perfectly balanced, because the demand and intensity are always changing.

I am writing this chapter in early January right after the flurry of the holiday season. Any person, mothers especially, knows how jam-packed the holiday season can be. There are gifts to buy (which in itself requires a certain degree of thought and planning), parties to attend, cookies to bake, presents to wrap, holiday cards to mail out, lights to hang, decorations to set up, magic to make, and if you've got kids, they're out of school, which means routine is thrown out the window. The holiday season brings with it merriment, cheer, joy, and a super-duper full mental load.

This is the perfect example of truth number one: *There are seasons and circumstances of life that impact the amount of energy and effort required to manage the mental load*, because there's just more going on. This is true for the holidays, birthdays, a move, the birth of a baby, sickness, job changes, renovations, work projects, and so on. The exciting, expected, unexpected, normal, seasonal, blessed, and tragic parts of life will all affect the mental load in some capacity, typically making it heavier, even if it's temporary.

Since the demands of the mental load are regularly changing, even if you have a system in place that works for who does what, this system will not permanently stay balanced. Distributing the tasks of the mental load is not one and done, because life will throw your system a curveball, requiring you and your partner to make tweaks and adjustments. Think of it like this: The next time you and your partner encounter one of these heavier seasons of life, who takes the extra tasks on? Do they default to you? Your partner? What does this look like?

I ask you these questions sort of rhetorically to make my point, which is that because this first truth exists, couples have to learn how to be able to navigate these heavier times without one partner picking up the bulk of it or balls getting dropped because the lines of communication break down.

I also point this out to normalize the experience of being at a cruising altitude with your partner and then hitting another bout of turbulence. You and your partner should learn to expect the unexpected and recognize that it doesn't mean that something is wrong with your system, your relationship, you, or your partner, but rather that you and your partner have to get really good at touching base with each other regularly (more on this to come) and making adjustments.

Truth 2: The distribution of responsibilities won't be fifty-fifty, but it should feel fair.

Every family has a unique set of circumstances. I have no clue what your values are, what your finances look like, and what amount of struggle, hustle, and grit is required for you and your family to make it in this world, which is why understanding this second truth is so important. You and your partner do not need to aim to have a fifty-fifty split when it comes to the responsibilities of the home and family, but I assure you, it's important that you discover what feels fair to you both.

Why not the fifty-fifty split? Well, because if you have a partner like mine who travels, this is an impossibility. Sometimes I hold dang near all responsibilities. Or if either you or your partner does shift work, is deployed, travels, or works multiple jobs, it may not make sense to have a fifty-fifty division of labor. You and your partner have your own unique situation that requires you to decide what feels fair given the amount of time and energy each partner has.

However, you must know that when either person in a partnership feels something is unfair in the relationship, this is when resentment and dissatisfaction occurs. There is a simple theory in psychology called *social exchange theory*, which is essentially an economic concept applied to relationships. It goes like this: People weigh out (consciously or unconsciously) the costs and benefits to being in a relationship. When the calculation results in an inequitable partnership, they are more likely to feel dissatisfied and unhappy and to exit the relationship. It's common sense. Yet, after years of being in a relationship, as we settle into our routine and devote less time to wooing each other, we can lose sight of this very powerful idea.

HER PERSPECTIVE

I am overwhelmed, bitter, and resentful. I feel invisible and less-than. Slowly, I am finding myself not wanting to interact with him because I get frustrated by his ignorance to my efforts and load.

Especially after having kids, I find myself frustrated with my husband when he's only responsible for himself but I'm ultimately responsible for the house, kids, and myself. It makes me feel unappreciated and taken for granted sometimes.

The tricky part of this truth is that "fair" is subjective. What may be considered fair to you may be unfair to your partner. Or you may feel it's fair in one moment and then you see more dirty cups on the bedside table and wet towels strewn on the floor and all of a sudden it doesn't feel so fair anymore. In chapter 19 you will be provided with the Better SHARE Agenda (Scheduled Home and Relationship Effort) where you will be prompted to regularly check in on feelings of fairness. This is an important checkpoint because fairness is a moving target. When the load increases, what is fair will also need to adjust. This requires that you and your partner get good at regularly negotiating fair without descending into defensiveness, tit-for-tat competitiveness, or just plain arguing.

A lie: Money is the default currency of the mental load.

Something that comes up often in my community is that women who are stay-at-home mothers (SAHMs) or who work part-time feel like they don't have a right to ask much of their partners because they don't make as much money. I want to be clear: Life costs money. I saw a reel recently where a guy was joking that everything costs $1,000. You go get a coffee: "That'll be $1,000." You go to a movie: "That's $1,000, sir." It doesn't feel that untrue. Life is expensive. When I spoke with men about the mental load, I asked them, "What stirs up defensiveness in you about the mental load conversation?" And one man said, "Don't forget: Doing all that we do and having all that we have costs money." Yes, we do need to remember that. It's important to honor *all* the contributions each partner makes to keeping a family functioning smoothly. You wouldn't be able to eat, sleep under a roof, or participate in modern life without money. I just want to also add this: Don't forget if she didn't do it, you'd be paying someone else to (which costs money) or you'd be taking care of it yourself (which costs time and energy). This sticking point is worth hashing out.

The issue becomes when money equals power in the relationship to the point that one partner starts to feel powerless because of their earning or lack of earning. The currency of our family and home life should not be money. The currency should be *time* and *energy*.

Let me give you a hypothetical.

- Partner A works one hour per week and makes $2 million (I'm being extreme on purpose).
- Partner B works sixty hours a week and makes $50,000.

Here's the question: Should Partner B have to carry the bulk of the labor at home because they make less money, even though they have less time and probably less energy? I would hope you'd say no. That's not realistic, sustainable, or even close to fair. That's a recipe for resentment.

HIS PERSPECTIVE

I know that I don't earn privileges just because I leave the house for work. That doesn't make my contribution harder or bigger than hers. We both have long days.

HER PERSPECTIVE

It seems like my husband thinks that if he's earning money, then his job is done and he's fulfilled his obligation.

The other problem with making the currency of the mental load money instead of time and energy is that most of the work related to maintaining a home and family is unpaid. To be blunt, this really sucks about Western society because we tend to equate value with money, so when something doesn't pay, it seems valueless. This couldn't be further from the truth, considering that someone has to hold down the fort, instill values, feed the family, keep up the house, manage the schedules, and so on in order for the other partner to concentrate on their work. In most families, both partners work in some capacity, so, again, time and energy over earnings becomes really essential to understand or else the partner making the most money will always feel entitled to do less. If having a family is important to *you*, then all the responsibilities and tasks required to care for said family should be viewed as essential as the other requirements to maintaining a family, like earning money.

I imagine this concept can make some people's heads spin Beetlejuice-style. It can be tricky to detach from the "money is the most valuable thing" mentality. So, let me give you one more piece of information. A recent survey of two thousand American women with kids ages five to twelve found that these women work an average of ninety-eight hours per week.[1] On average, the moms started their day at 6:23 a.m. and ended their day at 8:31 p.m. with approximately 1.7 hours of free time. Different sources estimate that a SAHM's salary would be anywhere between $117,000 to $198,000. I would argue that this number could be even higher if you accounted for the emotional labor that makes up a large portion of the mental load. SAHMs (or dads), you're working your butts off at an hours-equivalent of two and a half full-time jobs.

I want to add a quick note on energy. There are individual differences in people's energy levels. For example, my husband can't sit still and he's not a highly sensitive guy (I mean that in the highly sensitive person language—Google it if you're curious), which means his capacity isn't as impacted by his sensory system. Therefore, he's a pretty high-energy guy. However, if he gets crap sleep, he needs a power nap or else he doesn't function as well. I have high energy; however, I have a highly sensitive sensory system, which can wear me down quickly. But I can function on less sleep.

Consider your energy and your partner's; I bet they are different. Consider how you can factor this aspect into how you share the load and how you offer each other opportunities to recalibrate. You can use this energy checklist to quickly find what drains your energy versus what fills it.

THINGS THAT DRAIN YOUR ENERGY:

1. Overcommitting and saying yes when you mean no.
2. Constant multitasking without breaks.
3. Making decisions.
4. Remaining patient in the heat of frustrations.
5. Negative self-talk or replaying conflicts in your mind.
6. Taking on everyone else's problems (emotional contagion).
7. Skipping meals, hydration, or rest.
8. Scrolling social media.
9. Cluttered spaces that add to overwhelm.
10. Not speaking up about your needs and feeling resentful.

THINGS THAT FILL YOUR ENERGY:

1. Setting clear boundaries and protecting your time.
2. Engaging in activities that light you up (hobbies, exercise, reading).
3. Spending quality time with supportive friends or family.
4. Deep breathing, stretching, or meditation.
5. Exercising.
6. Getting enough sleep and eating nourishing foods.
7. Spending time in nature, sunshine, and fresh air.
8. Keeping promises to yourself.
9. Checking off small tasks to build momentum.

My point is this: If you're thinking that because you make the bulk of the income in the family, it's fair that you do less at home, you need to recalibrate your definition of *currency* from dollars to time and energy and then consider, "Do we have a comparable burden?" This shift in perspective is essential to being on the same page when discussing fairness in your relationship and how responsibilities are divvied up. Remember, it takes a lot to manage a family and run a household: Money is part of this, but not all of it. Work hard to appreciate each other's contributions to the family.

When you and your partner both buy into the two truths and a lie about the mental load, you begin to see that the solution to navigating it differently requires that you are on the same page, work together, share common language, and can communicate easily and frequently about the mental load without the conversation turning into a whole ordeal. In a nutshell, that's what this book is going to help you do.

get a load of this

Recap for the partner who carries the mental load at home

I hope this chapter normalized things that you may feel related to the mental load, like why you can't ever seem to get on top of things for good! Now you understand that it's because the demand and intensity of the mental load is always changing. I also hope that dispelling the lie helped you to find some language and assurance that you, too, deserve to have a partner in the home, not just a helper.

Load up on self-reflection. I want you to consider what fair looks like for you. It's easy to just say, "I want an even split," but that may not be realistic. Try to define what distribution would feel good given your life circumstances, what would free up some space in your mind and life, and what would result in more feelings of warmth and connection in your relationship.

Recap for the partner who carries less of the mental load at home

I hope that this chapter also normalized for you the reality that life will regularly change the intensity and demand of the mental load and that it helped to explain why your partner may often feel like the mental load is never eliminated. I promise you, your partner isn't trying to make things more difficult than they need to be; it's just that home and family life requires a ton of management, thought, and planning.

Load up on self-reflection around what fair would feel like for you. If you've subscribed to the lie that money is the main indicator of who should do what around the home, what you define as fair will be influenced. There is effort and output when working both inside and outside the home, so think about what feels like a fair distribution given effort, time, and energy expended. If you still struggle with the "dollars over time and energy" mentality, I encourage you to reflect on where this comes from. What has reinforced this belief in society, in your relationships, and in your past experience? And ask yourself, *Is this belief worth holding on to if it means disconnection in my relationship?*

CHAPTER
4

the weight of it all

Whenever I do interviews on the topic of the mental load, one of the most common questions is "Why do you think that it's most often carried by women?" I want to lay out some clear and simple reasons why I believe this is the case and how it gets so heavy so quickly. This chapter is key for understanding later sections of this book. So, if you're a skimmer, I ask that you slow your roll and take this part in.

How'd We Get Here?

One of my rock-bottom moments with the mental load occurred when our two kids were toddlers. It's a little fuzzy, but Effie was probably five and Roy was two and a half, and I was notorious for trying to do it all without asking for or expecting much help. It wasn't working out so well for me, and I was at my wit's end. I looked at Chad and said, "Just take them somewhere. I need to be alone." For fairness, since Chad doesn't have his own book to defend his position, I almost never asked for this. He was willing—maybe passively willing (more on this concept later) but willing nonetheless—but I just didn't make my needs known very well. That day I did, and he decided he would take the kids to the community pool and I would meet them in a couple of hours (my big mistake was agreeing to meet them; I should have just enjoyed some time to myself). I promptly disappeared and probably sat and stared at a wall for the next thirty minutes while they prepared to leave the house.

As I walked up to the pool, it's as if time slowed and the kids sensed my very presence, like the velociraptors in *Jurassic Park* hunting down their prey. As they saw me approach the large metal gate, their heads snapped toward me and their faces immediately shifted from glee to misery. I saw their mouths open and braced myself for the onslaught of tears and complaining that I was about to encounter. These were some very unhappy kids. Effie looked up at me and groaned, "I'm starving!" Followed up by Roy's "I am *soooo* hungry."

Turns out Chad didn't pack snacks, towels, or a change of clothes. He did take sunscreen, so at least we didn't have two cranky lobsters on our hands.

And I realize you may be distracted by this story because you're wondering one of two things: (1) Didn't I see this episode of *Bluey*? I assure you this really happened and years before *Bluey* was a thing. But when our family watched that episode, we nearly died laughing. (2) Isn't it common sense to pack all those things? Shouldn't he have known?

For sure he has responsibility here, too, and he thought the community pool provided towels, like a luxury resort or something. But that's not the point I want to draw from this story, so hold tight. The point is that I had packed the diaper bag, the water bottles, the snacks, the towels, and the change of clothes every single dang time, which meant that these tasks were never on Chad's radar. I realized I had single handedly taken on the lion's share of the "kid stuff" for so long that this guy didn't even know that snacks were the number one rule for toddler survival. Men are really good at holding on to only the most relevant information in their minds and ditching the rest. Think about it: Ever notice how when you verbally list items for the grocery store, after three or four items, they tell you to just make a list?

When you take something on, realize he may not use up his precious brain space worrying about it. This is one of the three reasons the mental load gets heavy so quickly and usually falls on women.

1. Piling on Precedents

The concept of piling on precedents goes like this: Early in your relationship you likely did things for your partner out of love and care-taking. Perhaps you even clicked right into the same patterns of what you saw growing up without realizing it. So you merrily went about your relationship loving on your partner by doing things like surprising them with the cologne they were out of, stocking their underwear drawer, buying his family gifts for the holidays, RSVPing for parties and buying the presents, or taking on the laundry responsibilities, because "I've got you, babe." This is all well and good, but over time these gestures of love add up. And remember what I said previously: When they're taken on by you, they're likely removed from his mind—therefore, they become yours for-ev-errrrr (*Sandlot* style).

There are ways to walk this back, but the most common outcome is that these tasks get absorbed by you. Women, we are the Bounty quicker picker uppers, because we are super absorbent. We just soak up all the extra tasks without—and this is key—ever really talking about it. Which means that the task becomes or remains invisible. Eventually, we become so saturated, we fall apart or break under the weight of it all.

Now, fast-forward a bit and you welcome your first baby into the world. Certainly, this is an exciting time, but it's also a time when responsibilities increase exponentially overnight. And guess what—most of them fall on the woman, for various reasons. So, you enter into parenthood with a full plate of invisible tasks and then pile on a ton more and, voila, you've got a very full mental load.

Why do we do this? Well, one reason is love. Another is that, as women, we're designed to nurture our relationships. This isn't always a popular statement to make, but allow me to expand on this a bit. Let's just say, in some ways, the game is a bit rigged.

2. The Game Is Rigged

Part of the answer to why the mental load tends to fall mostly to women can be found at the intersection of biological and social (including society at large and experiences at home) factors. I want to be clear: It's not just one of these two. It's both of them. And, as I'll keep reminding you throughout this book, there are vast individual differences among people.

A major reason that the mental load tends to fall more often to women is that women are socialized to be the caregivers in relationships. This socialization occurs at a young age both inside and outside the home, and oftentimes the message that is sent—and that we receive loud and clear—is that we are to *self-sacrifice for the sake of relationship preservation.* We must be the ones to give of ourselves in order to nurture, love, and care for others.

Men, on the other hand, are often socialized with a different message: *Your role is to provide security—both financial and physical.* I'll never forget reading in *The Boy Crisis* about how men are socialized with a belief system that their very lives are disposable when the security of others is at stake.[1] Meaning they should self-sacrifice for the preservation of women and children. Again, I'm painting with very broad strokes here. And you may be thinking, *My partner won't take the trash out, but you're telling me he would throw himself in front of a bullet for me?* Well, yeah, maybe.

You see, part of this socialization has to do with where value is attached. Historically, men have been valued for bravery and wealth, whereas women have been valued for attractiveness, how well they keep up their home, and how they care for others. This socialization affects us outside of our awareness and is deeply woven into the fabric of our lives. I get that these concepts can seem archaic; even writing this, I'm cringing. But our socialization is like an undercurrent that exists and requires us to do some excavating in order to examine how we're impacted by it and then choose to intentionally swim against the current in order to reshape the effects on our lives and relationships. I mostly want you to be aware of these in order to understand yourself and your partner better. When we understand how we tick, we can better step into empathy, understanding, and cooperation.

Now, layer this societal influence with what occurs in your home and what was reinforced. Some homes worked to go against the grain of what was happening outside the home, and others, well, just reinforced the same messages. What we see our caregivers model sets the stage for what we expect in our relationships later on from both ourselves and our partners.

Now, let's add in one final domain. I'm not going to get too in the weeds on this one, but it's important to mention. Men and women have brains and hormones and strengths that are different. Remember, individual differences exist, so I'm speaking in generalizations. For example, "In the brain centers for language and hearing, women have 11 percent more neurons than men. The principal hub of both emotion and memory formation—the hippocampus—is also larger in the female brain, as is the brain circuitry for language and observing emotions in others."[2]

Furthermore, when studies on emotional intelligence have been conducted, it's been shown repeatedly that women rate higher in two domains: empathy and others awareness. Empathy is the ability to relate to and understand the emotions of people around them, which makes them more likely to help. And others awareness is the ability to notice nuance in the emotion, body language, and expression of emotions. Have you ever noticed that you may have to cry in order to get your partner's attention, or just get really riled up? There is actually evidence to suggest that this is because men's brains take longer when interpreting emotion. In terms of emotional intelligence, men tend to rate higher on emotional control (regulation) and well-being (psychological health, positive outlook, and a sense of purpose).

Additionally, women's brains change in meaningful ways when they become mothers. Neuroplasticity is our nervous system's ability to change in response to external and internal stimuli by reorganizing its structure, functions, or connections.[3] In simple terms this means our brains can change due to different experiences and due to our environment.

When mothers' brains are studied, we see that reproduction-related brain plasticity (aka changes) occur in specific areas related to caregiving, such as these:

- **Reward/motivation:** Mothers get hits of feel-good chemicals when they hold their baby or when their baby smiles at them.

Rats have been shown to prefer pup suckling over getting a dose of cocaine[4]—that's how strong this dopamine and oxytocin hit is.

- **Salience/threat detection:** This helps the mother remain vigilant to potential threats to her baby as well as helps appraise emotional expressions of the baby so that she can attend to its needs.[5]
- **Emotional regulation:** Mothers are better able to regulate their emotions in order to deal with the intensity of their baby's outbursts and needs.
- **Social cognition:** This helps the mother have the ability to empathize with the mental state of the baby.

These changes are understood to be adaptive and necessary in order to help the mother and infant bond and to ensure the survival of the child. However, it also offers some explanation as to why mothers especially tend to experience some of the most drastic changes after birth compared to their partners. I know that all too familiar feeling of "my life has changed and his has remained the same." After becoming a mom, we feel this in so many ways, from worrying about the most insane circumstances under which harm could come to our babies to obsessing over the smallest details of their care because we just adore these children so much and have a primitive desire to protect them.

So why even bring this stuff up? I can just hear the cries of "So it's just that we're wired differently—that's it, is it? This isn't satisfying at all!" or "So you're just excusing my partner's behavior?" Not at all. I bring this up in order to offer a deeper understanding of how we tend to fall into these roles with seemingly no effort at all. We are socialized to be caretakers. We are wired to be caretakers. In terms of carrying the bulk of the mental load, the game is rigged.

3. Intensive Mothering

The term *intensive mothering* was a complete aha moment for me when I was doing research for my first book. It was just like learning there was the term *mental load* that captured an experience that I felt was uniquely mine and generalized it and offered me a sense of comradery with the rest of the female population. Intensive mothering was devised and researched by a sociologist named Sharon Hays in 1996. The term is sometimes referred to as *intensive parenting* as fathers are absolutely being pulled into this way of parenting more and more, but still, the impact of intensive parenting hits moms the hardest. The intensive mothering ideology is basically this: Mothers should expend an inordinate amount of time, money, and energy raising their children.[6] I get why you may think, *Of course, why wouldn't I?* But all you have to do is look back one generation (maybe two) to see that it wasn't always this way.

I remember asking my mom once, "What did you do when you had a question about parenting?" She said, "I just called one of my friends and did what they did." I know this isn't entirely true, because my parents—like many boomer parents—were some of the earliest adopters of a more intensive parenting style. It's just that millennial and Gen Z parents took it up a notch. If you asked a millennial parent or Gen Z parent the same question, the answer would be totally different: *I'd probably scroll my favorite parenting experts on TikTok or IG, listen to a podcast or twelve, read a self-help parenting book, or take a course.*

I'm not picking on these generations; I'm a geriatric millennial—we perfected this trend. In fact, the millennial generation is obsessed with self-improvement and with being their best selves and spend more than twice the amount of money on personal care and improvement than any other generation in history.[7] But the sheer amount of information at our fingertips coupled with the desire to be cycle breakers and repair and not repeat any big- or little-T traumas experienced in our own childhoods can make parenting in this day and age *very* laborious, exhausting, and well . . . intense.

Intensive mothering has five major defining features. See if any of these feel familiar to you.

1. **Essentialism:** the belief that mothers are the most important or essential parent, that we are the best ones for the job (anything or anyone else is second best or worse)

2. **Fulfillment:** the belief that parents should be completely fulfilled by their children (the whole "you complete me" belief)

3. **Stimulation:** the belief that involved parents should provide consistent intellectual stimulation for their children ("Oh, Johnny plays in his Montessori playroom with sensory bean bins to enhance his creative development.")

4. **Challenging:** the belief that parenting (done right) is hard and draining[8] ("If it feels hard, you're doing a good job.")

5. **Child-centered:** the belief that children are at the center of family life and parents revolve around them (aka, the kids are the sun. This is very different from European countries, where kids are expected to join into adult life)[9]

I'm sure it's helpful to see this concept articulated and explained, and I'd bet you feel it in your life. The constant onslaught of information, pressure to parent with such focused intention, and images of near perfection to compare yourself to is exhausting. Intensive mothering is a major factor in the increase of mental load because parenting with this amount of hypervigilance takes a ton of energy and time. Simply put, parenting in this way just adds more to your plate.

I'm not suggesting that you sacrifice your kids' well-being in order to take some things off your plate, but rather examine your relationship with those five beliefs that make up intensive mothering and see where you can make some adjustments. Your relationship to those five beliefs is what will predict the impact intensive mothering has on your life.[*]

But just calling these areas out and raising your awareness to them can help you think about how you want to make minor shifts. Even slight changes to how you relate to these five areas will have an impact. I also hope that calling this out can help you to have self-compassion, because parenting is tricky. If you're a nondefault partner reading this, I hope you can see how much this adds to your partner's plate and also

---

[*] I write extensively about this in my first book, *Love Your Kids Without Losing Yourself*, if you want to delve deeper into this concept.

that it lends some insight into why she may approach parenting with such high standards.

If you think about it, the three areas I described throughout this chapter make it not such a big surprise that women tend to be the ones noticing, worrying about, and caring for the members of the family as well as the home. I don't spell all this out in order to offer up an excuse for men or women or to say, "Well, there it is, folks, deal with it." I do it so you and your partner can have a greater depth of knowing and understanding how much the mental load can change relationships.

Which brings us to another major way that women are generally more affected by the mental load.

A Drop in Desire

Another result of a mental load that maxes out willpower and cognitive energy is that it crowds out the mental space for other things. One very important thing that gets crowded out is sex, particularly for women. I surveyed 536 women about how the mental load impacts their desire for sex, and they were asked to respond to the question "To what degree does the mental load impact your desire for sex?" Seventy-five percent of the women told me that the mental load has a significant impact on their desire. Here are just a few of the qualitative statements from women in the study:

- "The mental load makes me feel so tired I don't have energy for things that would benefit my marriage, like sex, exercise (so I'm a better me and wife), and patience."
- "It's hard. I am lonely because I feel like I don't have a partner. It impacts our sex life. That is all we fight about and our connection and relationship suffer."
- "I am tired all the time and I am not in the mood for sex, and I think he feels a little neglected."

I'm sure you're not surprised. How could it *not* impact desire? If you're a man reading this, I hope knowing the connection between sexual desire and the way the mental load is distributed and responded to makes you feel empowered and enlightened.

The research on the impact of the mental load on sexual desire is just beginning, but there is already support for what feels inherently true, which is that the more inequitable a relationship feels, the less desire a woman will have toward her husband.[10] Furthermore, another study looked at the perceived equity in a woman's relationship and her feelings of desire toward her partner as well as her general desire overall. The findings were very telling, revealing that a woman's desire toward her partner was impacted negatively the more inequitable she perceived the relationship, but her overall generalized desire was not.[11]

What does this mean? Well, it means that (for this sample) women aren't uninterested in sex or frigid—they are just uninterested in sex with their husbands when their relationships feel unfair.

There are three reasons why the mental load may be impacting your sexual relationship, and I want to help you understand exactly what they are. Let's do this (truly, I can't wait to include as many innuendos and puns as possible). Before I get into the details, I want to be clear that my suggestions throughout this book are for couples who are in a relatively healthy relationship and where absolutely no form of abuse is occurring. Additionally, forcible sex or any unwanted touching against your will is a major red flag and I encourage you to seek professional support.

The mental load may impact your desire for sex in three ways:

1. **You don't find your man-child sexy.** When you feel like your partner is not a partner but rather another person in your home adding to your load, creating more messes, criticizing your dinner, unable to figure things out on their own, not taking responsibility for their fair share, and spending their free time not connecting with you but playing video games or scrolling on their phone, they're going to seem like a man-child. And this does absolutely nothing for desire. When you decided to join your lives together, you didn't think you'd be getting into a situation where you are going to be tackling it all while your partner acts entitled to all your energy, care, and effort. This isn't a partnership; this is

parenting. Although a woman may put up with this, her feelings of excitement about jumping into bed with her partner will have likely dwindled, if she's even willing at all.

2. **Your head is full.** The second way the mental load impacts your sexual desire is that it crowds out room in your brain for sexy thoughts. Brains are our largest sex organ and we need to have room in our heads to get in a sexy state of mind. We also need to feel safe, secure, and relaxed to truly feel in the mood and desire sex. However, many women run around like revved engines, and by the time bedtime comes, they're so depleted physically and emotionally from carrying the weight of it all that their nervous systems have a hard time downregulating, which just leaves their minds racing. In order for women to be turned on for sex, their minds have to be turned off.[12] Plus, it's irritating to be in bed with your head spinning and have your partner expect one more thing from you.

3. **Your heart is not full.** Sex is often thought of as a separate piece in a relationship. Almost like you can surgically carve it out and the relationship can still exist, fairly intact. Like the appendix of relationships, if you will. However, your relationship health and connection will impact how safe you feel to engage in the sexual relationship just as the health of a sexual relationship will impact, for some, how connected they feel in their overall relationship. The important thing to remember is that sex is a piece of the whole of a relationship. It cannot be removed without other parts being impacted, just like the other parts will impact your sex life.

HER PERSPECTIVE

It feels like I'm mothering not only my child but also my husband. I have to constantly remind him to do basic tasks such as feed our son when he's looking after him. It's the opposite of sexy.

I feel exhausted and have very little desire for sex.

The resentment is high. I am starting to dislike my husband because I feel like I'm parenting another human. I feel like his mom. I'm not intimately attracted to him right now.

I am overwhelmed and resentful that a grown man who is wildly capable at his paying job seemingly cannot figure out the tasks and planning that need to happen at home. It makes me think of him as another kid to take care of and I have the ick.

I resent feeling like I have to mother my own spouse. I do not feel as though we have a partnership at all. I am a maid, nanny, means for sex, and nothing more. It makes me closed off emotionally to him and like we are just roommates.

One of the things women need in their relationship is to feel like they have a reliable partner. This produces a sense of security and feeling that they are loved. Sex is vulnerable. Giving your entire self to someone else is a big deal. A woman in a relationship with a partner who responds in the following ways isn't going to feel safe or loved in a relationship.

- He gets defensive when she shares her heart, and says, "It's never enough for you, is it?"
- He dismisses her overwhelm, just telling her, "Your standards are too high."
- He resists taking initiative: "I'm tired, just tell me what to do."
- He deficit defaults when she comes to him with a need, saying, "I guess I'm just not enough."
- He outright refuses to join in and participate in the family and home life.

Maybe this is occasional rather than a constant experience, but I would bet if this woman were totally honest, she would say that it's hard to work up the emotional energy to engage in sex with her partner. To feel really turned on, you have to be able to surrender to some extent. And if she is treated this way, she may not feel turned on, she may feel too unsafe and vulnerable, or she may feel annoyed or even recoil at her partner's touch. This is not an ideal situation for a healthy sexual relationship.

HIS PERSPECTIVE

We almost never had sex and definitely not enough time together. I felt criticized by her a lot and this grew into resentment.

Your desire can be directly impacted because you're weighed down cognitively, physically, and emotionally (the Triple Threat) from the mental load, crowding out space to get in a sexy state of mind. Or your desire can be affected indirectly because your partner isn't meeting your needs or expectations around the mental load, which creates a feeling of insecurity and inability to rely on your partner. Either way, the mental load has a major effect on desire, and if you hope to have a healthy sexual relationship, this is an important piece to consider.

Part of moving your relationship to a place where it feels fair and mutually fulfilling requires getting really good at talking about your relationship, or even difficult topics, without it leading to an argument. The next chapter will address how to get better at this and offer some general guidelines for successful communication.

get a load of this

I like to say, "When you define it, you can dominate it," which means when you define an experience, it empowers you to do something about it. I hope this section provided clarity on how you experience the mental load personally or offered a new perspective on your partner. My deepest hope is that you are inspired to have greater compassion for yourself and each other, because navigating our "go go go" world is demanding and stressful.

Load up on self-reflection. Consider how you subscribe to certain belief systems or participate in behaviors that contribute to your massive mental load.or lead to decreases in your taking more on. Talking about this with your partner and sharing your insights can be helpful. Furthermore, how do you feel the mental load impacts your sex life? This is a great question to reflect on personally or discuss with your partner. When you understand each other better, it increases a sense of knowing and being on the same page. This drives and deepens connection.

CHAPTER
5

can we talk?

When you're dating, "can we talk" almost always signifies the ending to a relationship. But in a committed relationship, "can we talk" is a necessity. Not having difficult discussions in relationships can actually be a sign of a problem because it almost always means someone is stuffing something or not expressing their needs. This means we have to shift our thinking as we work toward greater connection.

Unfortunately, many people grew up with family experiences where their parents weren't very expressive or communicative, so the discomfort of talking about "feelings" or difficult things is based on a deep and extensive history of learning that you shouldn't have to talk about your relationships. The idea that we only talk about our relationships when something is wrong is one of the most sabotaging beliefs in relationships. One iteration is *If our relationship is healthy, we shouldn't ever have to talk about it.* If you or your partner subscribe to these beliefs, here are some things you'll notice:

1. When you bring something up, you can see your partner's body language shift as if they're preparing for a fight.
2. You avoid bringing up conversations about your relationship

because they almost always end in an argument or you feeling worse off.

3. Your partner's (or your) knee-jerk reaction is to be defensive or convince you that what you're experiencing isn't real or valid.

If couples made the shift from a negative to a positive association with the phrase "can we talk," their relationships would immediately and dramatically improve.

Around fourteen years into our marriage, Chad and I were in a heated discussion. We don't really "fight." At least not in your typical sense with raised voices and over-the-top emotions. But during one tense discussion, I threw my hands up and said, "I just don't understand why you get so worked up when I need to bring something up." What came out of that conversation were two insights that shape how we approach talking about our relationships, which I believe apply to most couples.

We copy what was modeled and taught growing up. For Chad, what was modeled was that his parents either were not talking about their relationship at all ("It's all good here"), or they were having a major blowup and it was scary. There was no middle ground. Either everyone was chipper or things were a hot mess.

We take lessons to learn how to drive, we read the instructions on how to play a new game, and we watch YouTube videos on how to change a tire, but we almost never are formally taught about relationships. We just absorb what we see in and outside the home. And one message that is often received loud and clear is *talking about your relationship doesn't end well*. The natural conclusion is then, *well, I guess it's better to just never talk about it at all*. It's a misleading bit of logic because if you sweep things under the rug, does the mess still exist? Of course it does; it's just buried, likely getting grosser, embedding itself into the fibers of the rug. In addition, humans are wired with a survival instinct, which fuels this belief. While healthy conversations around relationships are rarely loud, emotional, scary, or all that memorable, if a child witnesses a conversation and it evokes fear, they may later be able to recall this memory. Unless intentional effort was made to process and talk about how to resolve conflict, it's likely you or your partner have learned that conflict is scary, and our survival instinct tells us to protect ourselves against disconnection and conflict, meaning many people avoid these conversations at all costs.

We have an overarching fear of abandonment. The second point is something that men tend to resonate with more than women: Unhappiness means they have failed, are not good enough, or are a terrible partner, and this has potential for abandonment. Chad and I have an extensive relationship history, seeing that we met when we were in high school. Between high school and marriage there were more breakups than I can even count, usually initiated by me (sorry, babe). This shared history of upset/unhappy equals abandonment created fear and worry in Chad that as soon as things became less than happy, I would leave. He was invested in me being okay. This fear of abandonment and disconnection is strong and exists to different extents in all of us, but when you add in a history, whether it's your shared history, past relationship experiences, or familial history, this fear is intensified.

Talking about your relationship has a way of summoning the relationship demons of the past and stirring up worry and anxiety around the health of your relationship and whether or not you'll be abandoned. It's important for couples to rewrite the narrative around "can we talk" so that these conversations become a normal rhythm in their relational life.

The Death Spiral

I sat at my desk and logged onto Zoom for one of my first interviews on the mental load. Vivian, a full-time working mom of two kids under the age of two, logged on. She was raring to go, and despite my nerves that I wouldn't have questions that spurred enough conversation and that I'd have to stare at a screen and endure an awkward silence, it never happened. She had things to talk about and, boy, was I glad she did. After the pandemic both Vivian and her husband of twelve years were now working from home. They had moved during the pandemic from the city to the suburbs in Illinois, which was a major change on top of now both being in the house all day together. When I asked her to describe where she and her husband get stuck with the mental load, she said,

> It's the invisibility piece that's hard. He will say, "Just tell me what to do," and so I did. And then he just hears all the ways he's not enough. It's frustrating. I want to be heard and he hears he's falling short. It's our death spiral. Then we get into a conversation where I feel like I'm justifying what I do so that he sees it and wants to help me, and then he doesn't get it and argues that he does more, and I'm like come on, just appreciate the doing. What I do doesn't negate your worth and what you do. We go round and round—hence the death spiral.

The wild part is that Vivian wasn't the only interviewee who referred to this as the death spiral. Probably because this experience sort of does feel like death, in part because the message that it sends is "You're too much for me" or "Your needs don't matter to me" or "I'm unreliable because you can't count on me to hear you out." These messages hurt and erode our feeling of trust in our partner and security in the relationship. I'll cover this later in the book, but people want to feel loved and secure in their relationships, and this response moves you farther from the goal line.

I call the tendency to hear a need or request from a partner and then respond with "I guess I just suck" (or some iteration of this) the *deficit default*. Part of why this happens is because one partner may feel responsible for the other's happiness and so an expressed hurt, suggestion, or unmet need feels like a personal failure. This makes the partner who goes into deficit default mode hypersensitive to feedback and they perceive almost any of it as criticism. However, this default response is like pouring salt in a wound. When someone works up the courage to come to their partner with an unmet need or a hurt, they're already vulnerable. Almost always their goal is to feel better in the relationship or to feel more connected, yet when they speak this need out loud and it's met with the deficit default response, they have only a few choices:

1. Get pissed and rage, creating a major argument. The result is that the need doesn't get met and the hurt is likely unresolved.
2. Spend the rest of the conversation reassuring their partner, making them feel okay, and not actually feeling heard. The result is their need is not met, the hurt is not resolved, and the hurting partner expends way too much energy.
3. Exit the conversation and stuff their needs, adding another block to the wall of resentment that's likely being built. Again, the result is that the need is not met and the hurt is not resolved.

With every deficit default response that takes a couple deeper into the death spiral, the less likely that partner will be to bring needs or complaints up in the future. This paves the road to resentment at a record pace. One of the primary reasons people respond this way is because of this belief: *If my partner has a need/hurt/request, it means I'm failing.*

HER PERSPECTIVE

The mental load has dissolved our connection. When I ask my partner for help or try to talk about it, they assume it's because I don't think they do enough. I live in a constant state of resentment.

Currently I am building resentment around the mental load because whenever I bring it up, he leaves the conversation feeling useless, which then means I have to reassure him that he's not useless.

A Necessary Shift

If you want to really move the needle in your relationship and learn how to navigate the mental load and the ups and downs of life together, then you need to deal with the way that you think about talking about your relationship. There are two lines of thought that sabotage being able to have regular or even difficult conversations in your relationship:

1. Relationships only get talked about when they are unhealthy or something is wrong.
2. If my partner has a need/hurt/request, it means I'm failing.

Somewhere along the way we've been fed a false narrative about love and relationships. We've been told things like *When you know, you know* or *If it's meant to be, it will work out.*

These narratives imply that relationships are instinctual and intuitive instead of intentional and requiring effort. These narratives have done our relationships a major disservice because they imply that relationships will just run themselves and if they run themselves into the ground, "Well then, it wasn't meant to be." Nothing could be further from the truth. Relationships require intentional and routine maintenance. We adopt this mentality in how we parent, in our friendships, and in our workplace, yet in our marriages we tend to lose sight of this important reality and feel bothered when something needs to be discussed. When we can get past the idea that relationships are supposed to run themselves without requiring any conversation or effort, we can lessen the shock value when things come up. Also, we can lessen the way we tend to take things personally when they do.

I encourage you to adopt a new line of thinking: *Your relationship and your partner always need something.*

If you work outside the home, your workplace probably has regular meetings. Why? Because there's always something that needs tweaking. If your work involves talking about financials, you may have a great month or quarter, but I bet your company is still looking to increase earnings. It doesn't mean that the company is going under or that you're failing as an employee; it's just that the company wants to be more profitable. And so you have meetings to review how things are going and to discuss changes and improvements that need to be made. If your boss encouraged you to expand reach in order to increase profitability, you wouldn't stand up and say, "I can't believe you'd say that. I guess I don't do anything right. I'm just the worst employee." Your boss would be irritated and this type of response would get old fast. At some point, you'd be fired for not having a mindset that embraced adaptability.

The same applies to our relationships. Instead of shrugging off our partner's needs or concerns, we need to work to become better for each other. At the risk of minimizing the shift some people will have to make to incorporate this belief system, ask yourself, *What's the big deal if my partner needs this from me? What's the big deal if my partner needs more words of encouragement or help around the house?* Our job as partners is to care for each other and ultimately to be malleable when the health of the relationship needs us to be. At the end of the day, when both partners embrace a growth mindset, that's when the relationship will really thrive.

If you can adopt the attitude that your relationship is always at a deficit, it will come as no surprise when your partner approaches you with a need or a change they'd like to see happen. It's not personal. You don't suck. It's just normal because—repeat after me—your relationship will always need something.

If you struggle to adopt this new way of thinking, consider these reframes to help you in the moment.

Thoughts	Revision
I'm failing as a partner.	It's normal for people to have needs. This has nothing to do with my failing.
They're going to leave me.	I'm safe. I'm listening. And I'm willing to work on this. No one is leaving anyone.
I guess I do nothing right.	Not everything is a personal attack. I can humble myself to see my partner's perspective.
It's never enough for my partner.	When I really reflect on what they're saying, is it that big of a deal, especially when it will serve our relationship?

Our relationships are always going to have shortages in different areas. It is impossible to score 100 percent in all areas of family and home life at the same time. Heck, it's hard to score 100 percent at any area of family and home life at any point in time. You have to accept the reality that it would be weird if you *weren't* falling short in certain areas because life is busy and the demands of work, home, family, kids, extracurriculars, holidays, unexpected stressors, and so on will regularly pull your relationship toward disconnection. Hence, your relationship will always need something, which means you and your partner have to figure out how to have conversations about what's going on in your relationship.

Navigating Tricky Conversations

There are entire books written on communication strategies and tactics, so I'm going to do my best to keep this very practical and direct. We'll start with some general guidelines for approaching conversations as a couple and then get into more specific strategies, especially around the deficit default response. Don't gloss over the following table—the approaches will drastically change how you communicate with each other.

Technique	Reason	Specific Tip
Strike when the iron is cold.	We tend to hold issues in until they carry over into everything or we burst. Try to bring an issue up when things are relatively good and when you're not hot and bothered. Otherwise, you run the risk of putting your partner on the defensive before the conversation has even begun.	Start with "Hey, I've been wanting to talk with you about something. You think you'd be up for it?"
Keep initial conversations short.	Talks that go on too long tend to get lost in the weeds. Try to keep your more serious conversations to thirty minutes or less and then schedule another conversation.	Use a timer if you can't seem to keep it brief.
Write things down.	Getting overwhelmed during difficult conversations is really common. When this happens, it's hard to remember your points or even why you're having the conversation.	Write down notes beforehand to help organize your thoughts and also to keep you from worrying about forgetting something you wanted to say.
Ask for reassurance.	This is a powerful regulator in relationships. Sometimes we just need to be told we're safe, loved, and that everything is okay.	Tell them: "I'm worried you're unhappy with me and thinking about leaving me. Can you reassure me that this isn't true?"
Do your best to avoid interruptions and listen to understand vs. respond.	It's common to craft your argument or rebuttal while listening to your partner's perspective and then when they stop talking, you provide your best argument. This undermines the communication process and often takes you deeper into an argument and further from truly understanding each other. Practice restating before moving on; this also slows the conversation down instead of racing quickly toward a danger zone.	Validate and restate before offering your perspective. It sounds like "It makes sense you're feeling frustrated. What I hear you saying is that you wish I would have checked in with you today before making plans. Can I tell you what I was thinking?"

Technique	Reason	Specific Tip
Take breaks if things get heated.	You wouldn't keep driving an overheated car, so why keep driving the conversation? It may feel uncomfortable but breaks can be necessary. When you take one, make sure to reassure your partner you will be back, and be specific about when that will be.	Let them know: "I'm feeling overwhelmed. Can we take a break and start again in thirty minutes?"
Fact-check your interpretations and assumptions.	If you're unclear about what your partner means, ask them to clarify. Don't assume.	Ask them: "Can you tell me what you mean when you say, _____?" Or "Let's stop and make sure we're understanding each other. This is what I'm hearing."
Use the defense attorney technique.	We have a tendency to explain our own perspective in many words, yet if we had to restate our partner's, we'd likely do it very quickly (if at all). Act like your partner's defense attorney and take turns restating each other's perspectives before moving into your own.	This works best if you take the same amount of time to explain back to your partner what they said as you do to explain your own perspective.

Navigating the Death Spiral

One of the most helpful techniques when navigating communication challenges that commonly come up in relationships is to move from content to process. Content is *what* you're talking about; process is *how* you talk about it. Most of the time, hurt comes from the process, not the content, and research has shown that arguments themselves are not bad for couples, but rather *how* couples argue is what ends up causing issues.

The death spiral is a process issue, not a content issue; it's the inability to talk about something without defensiveness and other unhelpful reactions. If you find yourself stuck in a death spiral or the deficit default is showing up, work to shift the conversation from content to process.

Another good practice is to keep discussions thematic versus getting into all the details and examples. This also helps you to avoid getting stuck in the weeds because inevitably when you're asked to explain something, every example becomes an exception. "Oh, well, *that* happened because of this." It's exhausting and frustrating. Here are two sample scripts as examples.

EXAMPLE 1:

Deficit default response: *So you say I do nothing around here?*

Response: *No, I know you have your own experiences and responsibilities. I'm simply saying there are aspects to our home and family life that I carry in my head that I think you don't. Mostly because you know I've got it. And the weight and amount of this has become unsustainable.*

Pulled into example: *Like what?*

Response: *I don't like having to prove this to you. But how many times have you thought about how our toilet paper stock is doing? How much space does holiday shopping occupy in your mind? Have you ever been distracted at work by the responsibilities you have at home? But my larger point is, I'm struggling because it's become too much for me and I need to know that we're on the same team with all of this and that I can count on you.*

EXAMPLE 2:

Defensiveness and deficit default: *I help, but it's never enough for you.*

Move to process vs. content: *I am not sharing this with you to blame you or criticize you. I am opening up my heart and letting you into my world so that we can handle this better as a couple. I am trying to reach out and talk with you about what I need.*

When you shut me down, it makes me feel like you don't

care about what I'm saying or how I'm doing. Like this isn't important to you.

Is your belief that I should keep things to myself? How am I supposed to approach you when something bothers me without you jumping to the conclusion that I think you're a bad partner?

TIPS FOR NAVIGATING DEFENSIVENESS AND THE DEFICIT DEFAULT

Tip	How to	Sounds like
Observe and ask	Notice the response and ask for it to be explained.	"You seem really upset by what I just said. What did you hear when I said this?" "You're getting heated. What's going on for you right now?"
Hedge defensiveness before it starts	You know your partner best, so use this only if you believe it will be received well. The agreement creates a momentary tension that can slow the defensiveness response. If they get defensive and agreed not to, they're breaking their end of the deal.	"I need to speak with you about something, but I'm worried you will get defensive. Can you handle this?" "You reassured me that you wouldn't get defensive and you are. What are you reacting to?"
Hold them accountable for the accusation	If a partner says things to you like "You're so sensitive" or "You just have too high of standards," the conversation can easily get away from you because these words hurt. When you hold someone accountable for their accusation, you require them to provide evidence for what they're saying and what "right" looks like for them.	"Okay, I heard that you think I have too high of standards. Can we talk about a specific example?" "Thanks, that helps me. So, what would lowered standards look like to you? Tell me your version of 'the right way.'"
Ask for the solution	Many times when people get defensive, they don't have a solution for how to do the conversation in a way where they won't be defensive; instead, they just don't want to have these conversations. Asking for a solution helps them rationalize their perspective and gives you guidelines.	"I'm going to have to bring things up to you from time to time. How can I do this without you getting defensive? We need a new plan."

Your Secret Communication Weapon

Reinforcing the idea that your partner and relationship always need something requires that you live it out. You may say you're all about talk, but when your partner approaches you with "can we talk" do you bristle, work up your best defense, and prep for a fight? You've got to walk the talk, my friend, and put this new belief into practice.

One of the best ways to do this is to schedule regular relationship talks. This strategy is not new. It's the foundation of my dad and my couples' course, Rock Solid Marriage, and other relationship educators have recommended having "state of our union" talks. This scheduling of regular relationship talks has some really powerful benefits.

1. **It normalizes talking about your relationship.** When you schedule regular relationship talks, you normalize the need to talk about your relationship. This reinforces a new mindset and will have the added benefit of improving your relationship because small issues will not fester and become massive problems that erode your connection, love for each other, and sex life.

2. **It shares the responsibility of relationship management.** Relationship management falls into the emotional labor category of the mental load. The majority of the time this work falls to women. Women tend to be the ones saying things like "Can we have a date night?" or "Can we talk?" Over time this responsibility can start to feel like you're the only one who cares about the health and happiness of the relationship. When you schedule a regular time to meet and talk as a couple, this means that this aspect of relationship management is shared between both partners. It also has an added benefit of the woman in the relationship feeling like she has an outlet to connect emotionally and that her partner is reliable and willing to show up for her and the relationship.

We'll get into practical ways to implement this meeting into your routine in a later chapter. But now that you understand the importance of making the mental adjustment around your relationship always needing something, it's time to dive into four areas you and your partner need to better share in order to make meaningful shifts around how the mental load is handled in your relationship. Each section will culminate in questions you will use in your relationship meeting to regularly check in with each other. Are you ready to learn how to find a better share? Let's get into it.

get a load of this

If you master the ability to create open lines of communication in your relationship, your relationship will change forever. If you're willing to sit and listen to your partner and hear their heart without diving headfirst into the death spiral of defensiveness and other poor communication patterns, your relationship will dramatically improve. This chapter is worth reviewing if this is new to you.

Load up on perspective and humility. The ease at which you and your partner are able to talk openly about needs, changes, and requests in your relationship is directly related to how well you depersonalize their requests, accept the belief that your relationship always needs something, and put in the effort to consider their perspective. If you struggle with the death spiral and the associated behaviors that take your relationship conversations off course, I encourage you to consider: Why do I think my relationship should run on autopilot forever, needing no changes, when almost nothing else in life works this way? Am I offended when the plants need watered? Am I put off when my kid needs a hug or a snack? Where did this belief come from and how would my relationship look different if I abandoned it?

PART
2

sharing is
caring

CHAPTER
6

SHARE PERSPECTIVE

what do we want?

Sharing perspective means that you understand each other's differences and work with them instead of resenting them.

One of my more recent guilty pleasures is listening to books in the rom-com category. Basically, the Emily Henry–esque books that are well written and funny, have great character development, and are easy reads that always end happily. They're beyond fun and I highly recommend this healthy mode of escapism. But when I reflected on why I loved these books so much, why they lured me in so quickly and scratched an itch I didn't realize I had, I recognized that part of the allure of these reads was that the men in them are unicorns.

It's the same conclusion I've drawn about Jamie in *Outlander*—these men are a wildly rare mix of masculine and feminine. They are masculine in all the ways you'd want: their sexual prowess, their appearance, their handiness, their toughness. Yet they're feminine in ways that are less commonly found in real life: Emotionally vulnerable and intelligent (but not needy) and highly expressive, they notice the small details about the woman they're pursuing, regularly incorporate this knowing into romantic gestures, and they pursue her with abandon. These men check all the boxes for what women are wanting in their relationships.

In many ways, the female characters are just as much unicorns as the male characters. They are sexually assertive, unemotionally "easy," and don't put any demands on the men. I mean, why would they? The men are doing all the right things. These rom-coms depict a really clear picture of what men and women want most in their relationships—the problem is, real life isn't scripted in the same way. We have hurts and worries and socialization written onto our pages, whereas these characters do not.

As I outline what men and women desire most in their relationships, you'll notice that both people want the same thing: to feel loved and secure. Yet the ways we want this expressed are very different. Please remember that this is a broad-stroke representation of men and women. Each person is different, and some aspects may resonate with you more than others; however, this information is based on psychological research and theory on differences in relationships.

Before I go deeper into this topic, I want to be clear about a few things. Talking about differences between men and women is out of favor. I'm not sure exactly why and I'm not going to speculate, but I believe that while we have more similarities than differences, ignoring the ways that we're different doesn't do us any favors. Some things that are different about us can become easily personalized: "My partner just doesn't love me" or "She's so emotional." Sometimes this isn't true but is instead due to the differences between men and women. I am asking that you transport yourself into your partner's perspective, and hopefully they do the same for you.

Different Means, Same End

I want to remind you again that men and women want the same thing—to feel loved and secure—even though they express it in different ways. When you depersonalize some of the behaviors that seem specific to your partner, you and your partner can come together to tackle the mental load as a team. Yes, you may be different. But different isn't bad, so let's maximize these differences and make them work for your relationship.

The first step is understanding the unique desires of each partner. Think of it like this: When you're the parent to more than one kid, you begin to realize the differences in preferences, personalities, and temperaments, and so you make adjustments to how you parent based on those differences. I bet some of you have even dug deep into certain qualities about one of your kids to gain insights into how to parent them. This is not that different from doing that with your partner in order to understand and know them better so you can navigate your relationship more successfully.

If you've signed up for an eternity together, why not learn how to maximize your relationship satisfaction and happiness? Part of how this is accomplished is by learning about each other and understanding how you each like to be loved and cared for. When couples don't embrace an attitude of wanting to mutually fulfill each other's needs and love each other in the ways they desire most, distance starts to develop and resentment takes root. Let me explain.

The Cycle of Unmet Needs

Couples get trapped in a cyclone-esque cycle of having needs that go unmet or misunderstood. Unfortunately, when couples get stuck in this cycle, their deepest desires end up getting sabotaged along the way.

Let me give you an example.

Whitney has a need for her partner to be reliable. She thought she married a guy who would take initiative around the house—after all, he lived on his own forever—but now it's like everything defaults to her. She's sick of it and feels invisible and like her partner isn't there for her. She pursues her need by asking for more help and telling her partner she needs him to take initiative. He receives her need as criticism: "I guess I don't do anything right. I'm a horrible husband." This is the response to the pursuit.

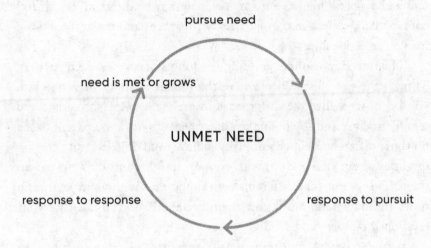

the cycle of an unmet need

pursue need

need is met or grows

UNMET NEED

response to response

response to pursuit

Now Whitney gets to decide what her response to him is. She decides to escalate her request to a demand in order to continue to pursue this need. The need is growing. This is disturbing his need for peace, and now he's feeling disrespected. She's feeling utterly invisible and unheard and unloved. As she pursues harder, he withdraws. He doesn't want to deal with it. She feels even more invisible and decides this time that, instead of escalating, she will withdraw too. A rift has formed. She is not feeling appreciated or pursued, nor does she feel that she has a reliable partner. He is feeling disrespected and just wants peace, and it's likely this isn't doing their sex life any favors. This cycle is called the *pursue-withdrawal cycle* and has been talked about in numerous books and in attachment theory—it's common but destructive.

Can you see yourself in this cycle? If so, there's hope. The rest of this book is about interrupting that cycle, specifically around the mental load, and getting to a place where both you and your partner are getting your needs met most of the time.

I want to explicitly address something before we move into the chapters on what women and men want in their relationship. You may read the chapters and say, "I already do that" or "My partner asks for that and I do it already. It's never enough." Hear me very clearly:

Sometimes we just want more of something. If your partner asks for appreciation, I bet you offer it, but maybe your partner just desires *more* of it. Try not to get caught up in defending what you do and instead step into trying to love your partner better. Think of it as math. In relationships, when it comes to needs and desires, usually we want something added to the relationship, subtracted from the relationship, or multiplied. When your partner comes to you with a request, think about it like that. Do they want something new added, something subtracted or removed, or do they want more of something you're already doing (multiplied)?

In the next two chapters, I am going to examine what women want most in their relationships and then what men want most. My hope is that these chapters spark some aha moments and help you both feel seen and understood. We often struggle to communicate clearly our wants and needs or we personalize our partner's requests by taking them as criticism instead of attempts at deeper connection. When it comes to caring well for each other, things really don't need to be that complicated.

get a load of this

Personal Power

You can discuss these questions with your partner or simply reflect on them yourself. Both uses will be helpful.

- Can you identify your unmet need cycle? What is the unmet need? What is your partner's response? How then do you respond? If you need to, draw this out so it's clear.
- Now try drawing out your partner's unmet need cycle, including your most typical response.
- If this unmet need cycle has been going on a long time, how has it impacted your relationship? Consider both your cycle and your partner's.
- How would you like this cycle to change? *Be specific.* If you say, "Well, meet my darn need," be clear about what it looks like to meet the need in the way you want. Think: If it were caught on camera, what would you see?
- Imagine some potential areas for change.
  - » What would happen if you asserted your need in a new way?
  - » What would happen if you responded differently when your need wasn't met in the way you wanted?
  - » What would happen if you received your partner's need with openness?

Better Together

If you're doing this with a partner, come up with one goal for disrupting the unmet need cycle. What can each of you promise to do differently from here on out?

CHAPTER

7

what does she want?

Women want three primary things in relationships:

1. **P**ursuit
2. **A**ppreciation
3. **R**eliability

Each of these three points to the same end goal: for her to know she is loved and secure, ultimately feeling reassured that her partner is there for her. If you're unsure how to care for the woman in your life, this section is for you. If you're unsure what you actually want from your partner, I hope this section will help you to be clearer about what you need. In an attempt to make these three areas memorable, I've used the acronym PAR for what both women and men want in relationships. The letters stand for different things, but the acronym is the same. In golf, par is the expected number of strokes an expert golfer should make on any given hole. If you hit par, you're doing pretty dang good. The same applies here.

Pursue Her

Common sense would tell us that our relationships will not be the same ten years in as it was in the beginning—yet it still comes as a shock when the romance seems nonexistent and we feel invisible to our partners. In the beginning of a relationship, men step outside their comfort zone to win over the heart of their beloved. They are more emotionally expressive, more vulnerable, and the way that they prioritize life puts the woman at the top, with everything else a far second. But once they've secured love, things start to recalibrate in a way that doesn't offer the same fairy-tale existence. Work obligations become primary, they don't express as much emotion, and the romantic gestures tend to fall by the wayside.

If you remember what I said previously about how our socialization impacts us differently, men are socialized to provide and protect. So, after they've secured love, they often slide right back into provide-and-protect mode, which means it's easier for them to sideline romance for these felt higher-order "duties."

Before you start to feel discouraged or get righteous on me—I've actually received a DM saying, "This is why I tell every woman I know not to get married"—as women, we do a similar thing. While we are really good at taking care of the needs of others, we do tend to get busier with other tasks of life. Maybe it's our job, the kids, or those stinking dishes calling our name, but our partner tends to fall lower and lower on the priority list as well. Yes, we still care for them, but our enthusiasm in how we express our interest in them likely shifts.

As women we have a deep desire to be pursued by our partners. We want them to put in effort, plan the dates, let us know that we are still desirable and that they want to spend time with us. Especially after kids, women can start to feel like they are the hired help but without the pay. This doesn't feel good, nor is it conducive to an exciting and mutually fulfilling relationship. And so, here are a few ways that you can specifically pursue your partner.

1. Pursue knowing her deeply.

Seek and strive to know her deeply. What makes her tick? What are her favorite things? What does she despise? Be a gatherer of information and ask questions that will help you to care for her in new ways and show her that you pay attention to her. Yes, you may be years into your relationship, but knowing one another never ends. We act like there's an end point, but with every day comes new experiences and these impact us, leaving us with new things to learn. Continue trying to know her on a deep level. When you take this knowing and translate it into action, watch your relationship radically change.

Here are some questions to get you started:

- What's something that has changed about you since we first met?
- What's something I used to do for you that you wish I still did now?
- If you could plan the perfect day, what would it look like?

2. Pursue having fun with her.

Fun is the antidote to your relationship falling into a rut. This one is so simple, yet relationships often fall victim to the monotony of routine. Rise, eat, drive kids all over creation, work, eat, drive kids all over creation, eat, sleep, repeat. You and your partner probably spend most of your time uploading and downloading information to each other about the logistics of life. It's not fun. You used to have fun together. It's time to remember how much you like being with each other. Work to pursue opportunities to incorporate more fun into your life together. When you do this, you create new experiences to talk about and laugh about. You also get to know each other in different ways, outside the confines of daily routine. When you pursue fun together you're also showing your partner that you enjoy being with her and desire to spend time with her.

Here are some practical ways to pursue fun together:

- Have a weekly game night together. Friendly competition always changes things up.
- Engage in a new hobby together or pull her into one of your

hobbies (women notoriously sacrifice hobbies after kids; encourage her to develop one or pursue one she has abandoned).

- Go to a comedy club (splurge) or watch a comedian together at home (save).
- Hang out with other couples. This changes the dynamic and breaks you out of your routine.

3. Pursue affection with her.

Women are often taught that a significant amount of their value resides in their appearance, and experience often supports this. I remember showing my husband a quote in a book I was reading by prolific relationship researcher John Gottman that said for women, shopping is "a matter of personal and genetic survival."[1] I had never thought of shopping in this way and that women would view it differently than men, but I think we can all agree that a woman's identity is defined and often judged by how she looks. The gist of Gottman's suggestion was that women have an evolutionary predisposition to be gatherers, and this, coupled with our keen memory for details, helps us to go out into the world and gather things that make our families feel safe and cared for. This sounds like "Oh, Chad would love this shirt" or "Roy needs more sweatpants." In addition, shopping and adorning herself is part of how a woman sets herself apart from others, how she secures love.

I realize these may seem like stereotypical ideas and that you may want to reject the idea that women are still caring this much about how they look; however, the deep roots of these influences remain. Because of this, affection often demonstrates that you find your partner desirable and attractive. That you see her beauty and it stands out to you and that you want her. Maybe your sex life isn't what you want right now, but if you're not pursuing her by letting her know how beautiful she is to you, you're missing a major opportunity and likely she's feeling unwanted. And feeling unwanted is lonely.

Also, I included the shopping bit to provide another perspective on a behavior that often gets criticized or made fun of. Her shopping behavior may be related to her desire to look attractive because that's what society expects of her and is an expression of how she cares for and loves your family. Unless she's putting your family in financial jeopardy, if you've been critical of this behavior, you may be doing more harm than good. Instead, thank her for making your house a home. Thank her for anticipating the needs of your family. And express to her your feelings of affection and attraction to her.

Here are some practical ways to express affection:

- Tell her how beautiful you think she is.
- Touch her when you walk by.
- Make eye contact with her across a room of screaming kids and smile.
- Tell her you appreciate how well she cares for your family and all the work she does to find the best stuff (food, tools, resources, extracurriculars, etc.).

Appreciate Her

My husband and I met in high school. I was the ripe old age of fourteen and he was sixteen (we didn't date that entire time; I have to say that or else I lose street cred). I grew up with a dad who had his PhD in psychology and created courses to help people with their relationships. That is to say, I had really mature (aka high) standards for my dating relationships. I remember telling Chad, who wasn't all that verbose, that I wanted him to make me more cards. Looking back, I'm so glad I did because I have a box full of cards he made me in high school on his computer. They're adorable and hilarious. What I realize now, that I couldn't articulate then, is that I needed more expression from him. I needed more words to let me know how he felt and what he appreciated about me. It took me years of marriage to finally pinpoint that what I needed from him was appreciation.

Women want to feel appreciated for all that they do to care for you, the home, your children, and generally what they contribute to the world. They want to know that they are visible and valued. We have a history of being seen as "less than" men, as our contributions to the home go unpaid and definitely undervalued. I'll let you in on a hint: We don't always love carrying the weight of being the family manager. So, appreciating what your partner does regularly and expressing it with sincerity makes a huge difference. In my survey of women, when I asked them what they need most when it comes to the mental load, the second most common answer was "appreciation and acknowledgment for all I do" (31 percent), after "my partner to take more initiative" (50 percent).

I've come up with the ultimate compliment formula that can help you to become a master at expressing appreciation to your partner. The more specific you are, the better your compliments will go. Please know, you cannot express too much appreciation. You will not make your partner's head big. You will not lose power. Don't be stingy with appreciation.

THE ULTIMATE COMPLIMENT FORMULA

$$\text{Observation} + \frac{\text{Positive Impact}}{\text{on Your Life}} = \frac{\text{The Ultimate}}{\text{Compliment}}$$

Here are some examples:

"I see how hard you work to make sure the house is always stocked with what we like [observation]. I want you to know this is such a gift to me. I always know we're taken care of and I don't have to worry about this part of life [positive impact]. Thank you."

"I see how much you worry about the kids [observation]. I always feel at peace knowing they will be okay because you have the bases covered. You're so good at this. Thank you for taking care of our family in this way [positive impact]."

HER PERSPECTIVE

Most of the time it's not even the work with the mental load, it's the invisibleness, the lack of appreciation and validation.

I just need my partner to breathe life into me sometimes with words.

Be Reliable for Her

John Gottman said women have two primary complaints in their relationships:

1. He is never there for me.
2. There isn't enough intimacy and connection.

I would consider both of these as falling into the category of reliability, which basically means consistency in behavior and performance, or being trustworthy. In a nutshell, are you going to do what you say you're going to do and be who you said you'd be?

As I stated earlier in the chapter, courtship behaviors often decline with a feeling of security: We've got each other, so now we can relax. Security is a great thing; however, the decline in effort elicits a feeling of being falsely advertised to in the dating process. We think, *I had a partner who would prioritize me above all else in the beginning, and now he won't even spend time with me over playing video games.* Or *He used to open car doors and make late-night runs to get me ice cream; now I can't even get him to take the trash out. He must not care about me.*

The thing that is important to realize is that these failures in reliability lead to feelings of being unloved and insecure in the relationship. This radically shifts the dynamic. Now, before you protest, I understand that there are two sides to every story, but you have to see this clearly to understand how disconnect occurs between you and your partner.

Being there for your partner may mean being someone she can depend on to help around the house, listening to her when she's upset, asking questions about her world and relationships, supporting her work inside and outside the home, knowing the kids' schedules so she doesn't have to carry that alone, and so on. It isn't just about the big stuff; it's about the day-to-day, which means that there are plenty of opportunities for her to feel like she's on her own without the partner she felt she was promised.

A common result of these disappointments, especially around the mental load, is that women take on the role as coach or manager, trying to coax their partner to do more, step up more, be the partner she needs. At first this may be well-received, but often this coaching becomes interpreted as criticism, which ends up causing major rifts in the relationship. She's taken on the deeply unsatisfying role of "parenting" her partner, and in his eyes, she's become the nagging mother. Neither partner is satisfied, and it makes sense if you feel like you're stuck in the revolving door like Buddy the Elf, going around and around until you feel like you're going to be sick. Of course, intimacy and connection are going to suffer when this happens.

When a woman feels dissatisfied in her relationship, she usually responds in one of two ways:

1. **Withdrawing:** This creates more distance between her and her partner. She tries to go inward in order to not be so hurt and then becomes cold. He feels this distance and bristles in order to protect himself (more on this in the next section).

2. **Escalating demands:** When a woman feels a lack of closeness and connection, she may make bids for connection. In an attempt to close the gap and feel loved and secure again, she pursues, but he reads it as criticism and responds with defensiveness or dismissiveness, and her hurt intensifies. She becomes more desperate and escalates, causing the pattern to continue. It's like a corkscrew; each turn in this pattern deepens into the cork. The couple is stuck and neither partner is getting what they want.

Interrupting this dynamic takes a little work, but when you can see it plainly for what it is, it makes it a whole lot easier. In fact, if you can recognize this in your relationship, you can start to shift it by being more of a reliable partner. Inevitably, in every relationship there are times when one partner has to step toward the other, making the first move, waving the white flag, and calling a ceasefire. You've got to disrupt the dynamic before it consumes your relationship, erodes your connection, and you forget what it felt like to be in love.

One of the most powerful ways to shift the dynamic with your partner is to practice something Gottman calls *emotional attunement*. He uses the acronym ATTUNE to spell out what this means.[2]

Attend: Give your undivided attention when she needs you. Put down your phone, drop your Xbox controller, look up from your laptop, and look her in the eyes.

Turn toward: My husband feels close to me when we're just in the same room, but I do not feel close unless we're engaged in meaningful conversation. Most women and men are similar in these two differences. So when she needs you, turn your body toward hers and look face-to-face. Do not just exist alongside her and expect her to feel connected.

Understand: The objective when she speaks should almost always be understanding. You may want to rescue her from whatever she's venting about, but instead seek to understand it better. Try asking questions and showing a genuine interest. If you feel confused about whether she wants a suggestion, ask, "What do you need from me right now?" Yes, it's that simple.

Nondefensively listen: If you're doing all this, work to temper your defensiveness. I promise you, being defensive will not get you anywhere. You don't have to agree with her, but you can seek to understand her feelings. There are always multiple versions of an experience; seek to hear and understand hers. If you feel overwhelmed or like you're overheating, ask for a break and then come back to the conversation.

Empathize: Empathy is understanding with emotion, feeling what the other person is feeling. This may feel like trying to speak a foreign language, but know that it will make her feel safe and heard by you, like you are interested in her, as I'm sure you are but she may not always feel. You can express empathy by better understanding her feelings, and you can do this by asking more questions or asking what she needs. You can even say things like "That must have felt _____" or "This wasn't what you expected" or "I can imagine you feel _____."*

When you practice these skills, you will be showing your partner that you are safe and predictable, and this facilitates more intimacy and connection. I cannot emphasize enough how important it is to continue to work toward being a more reliable partner.

Here are practical ways to demonstrate reliability.

1. **Maturity.** This means you may have to learn how to better control your emotions and stave off defensiveness when it's triggered. Do some work here; it will make a big difference.

2. **Deliverability.** If you say you're going to do something, make sure you do it. For example, if you said you're going to plan a date night, do it. Don't wait for her reminder; show her that you can take something on without her having to manage you every step of the way. Again, no one finds a man-child sexy.

3. **Consistency.** When you sometimes show up and sometimes don't or sometimes support her and sometimes don't, you seem unsafe. Be predictable and consistent.

4. **Availability.** Be present for her and emotionally available. Care about what she has to say and demonstrate your support.

---

* Gottman originally used "turn toward" to represent the *T*'s in ATTUNE but has since added "tolerance." For more on emotional attunement, visit The Gottman Institute online.

You've hit PAR!

Remember, both partners have the same end goal when it comes to their relationships: They want to feel safe and loved. When you're pursuing her, appreciating her, and being a reliable partner, you will foster a sense of security in her and she will feel loved. While this alone doesn't solve the mental load problem, it creates warmth and connection, which is a way better base to work from than distance and contempt.

get a load of this

Personal Power: Her

- When you think about PAR (pursuit, appreciation, and reliability), which one do you feel you need more of in your relationship?
- In what areas do you feel like your partner is doing a good job?
- If it were caught on camera, consider what ideal pursuit, ideal appreciation, and ideal reliability would look like from your partner.

Personal Power: Him

- Try to be as objective as possible: How would you rate your performance in each of these areas? Where could you improve?
- Which expressions of PAR feel easy for you to deliver on? Which ones are you unsure how to meet? Which make you feel uncomfortable?
- Which expression does your partner regularly ask for that you feel like you could do better on? Or are you not sure about how to do it in the way she prefers?
- What stops you or feels like a barrier to hitting PAR in your relationship?

Better Together

Talk together about some of the responses you had to the questions above. Share two or three things you notice that your partner does for you that hit PAR that you appreciate. Share one or two things you would like more of. Work to be clear when you describe this to your partner.

As you receive your partner's requests, explain back to them what you heard they're asking for. Offer a couple of ideas of how this change can be implemented in your relationship.

CHAPTER
8

SHARE PERSPECTIVE

what does he want?

Men want three primary things in relationships:

1. **P**eace
2. **A**ffection
3. **R**espect

Each of these three points to the same end goal: to feel loved and secure and to know that he is a good enough partner. If you are unsure how to care for your partner, this section is for you. If your partner drives you crazy because you feel like you don't understand why he responds the way he does, or why he disappears when you get emotional, or why he seems so sensitive to your request for change, this section is for you.

If you're the man in the relationship, I hope that this chapter does good by you and that it offers insight into why you feel the way you do and respond the way you do and helps you to get more of what you want in your relationship. Remember, if you hit PAR, you're on your way, but this section will enlighten you further. Keep in mind, I will talk in generalizations and themes, so if you find yourself pushing back against some of the points, that's okay. It may not all apply to you; however, this is based on physiological and psychological research and writings.

Give Him Peace

A common theme I see with couples is that their relationship tends to go smoothly as long as the female is happy. Light, airy, pleased, and overall pleasant. Ahh, a man's dream—no fuss, no stress. Remember when I described the rom-com books I've been reading, and how the female characters are rarely emotional, often tough, very fun, and sexually adventurous and uninhibited? Unfortunately, we don't live in a rom-com novel and it's not feasible to be light and airy all the time.

I was talking with one of my good friends who decided to go back to school to pursue her master's degree after supporting (and still continuing to support) her husband's very busy career for over two decades, and she said something along the lines of "It's like as soon as I get stressed out or need him to step in and support me, the wheels fall off. Really?! After all these years? I'm sorry I'm not easygoing right now. I have a lot on my plate." This is a sentiment I've heard echoed over and over from women I work with or speak with: When women experience more stress or are not "happy," men feel uncomfortable. Here's why:

1. Because too much emotion is confusing, scary, and unnecessary.

Have you ever noticed that when you get emotionally overwhelmed, your partner almost immediately goes into fix-it mode? If they don't, then I bet you've worked on this as a couple. It's a common stereotype about men and women's relationships that gets complained about all the time but not really analyzed. In many ways, it's often simplified, like "Men, get your act together." From a man's perspective, it just seems logical to cut through the emotional baloney and get to the solutions. He thinks he's helping. But she doesn't understand why it's so hard to offer some empathy and support. When she doesn't respond with a giant thank-you, he's confused, feels powerless, and likely is a little irritated.

In *The Male Brain* Dr. Brizendine breaks down the two emotional systems in our brains that work simultaneously but differently in men and women.[1] The two systems are the *mirror-neuron system* (MNS) and the *temporal-parietal junction system* (TPJ). The MNS is what helps you to register a look on someone's face and feel what they're feeling. This is called emotional empathy. The TPJ is the analyze-and-fix-it system; it searches for solutions. This is called cognitive empathy. The male brain starts to show preference for the TPJ system after puberty, and this system works hard to keep a wall up between emotions of the self and others. As Dr. Brizendine says, "This prevents men's thought processes from being *infected* by other people's emotions, which strengthens their ability to cognitively and analytically find a solution."[2]

I can relate to the experience of feeling like my emotions were an infection Chad was trying to avoid catching. Recently, I shared with him about a painful experience in a close friendship. He empathized with me for a while (he's gotten good at this), and the next time I brought it up, he said, "Just sounds like drama to me."

There is this tendency for men to push away the emotion and favor the logic. This isn't bad, even though we tend to label it as such, but we have to understand that this difference often stirs up misunderstandings and conflict in our relationships. Let me be clear with you both: You aren't better because you're more logical. And you aren't better because you're more emotional. Both of these skills are important; you're just different in this way, and you have to learn to cross over into each other's worlds, to complement each other with these differences versus just complain about them. Men, you will have to get comfy with emotions, and women, you'll have to learn that many men will be wired to fix things. It is well-intentioned, just not always what you need.

HIS PERSPECTIVE

I worry way more about providing financially than I do about messing up our kids. I don't mean that to sound harsh, but I just feel like it's my job to keep my family safe.

Now let's add another layer to this knowledge, which is the socialization of boys in our Western culture. We are often taught that boys don't cry, a man's job is to provide and protect, their worth is tied to their performance, and showing confidence and strength is paramount to masculinity.

I'd like to share two studies that shed light on men's emotional world. The first experiment is called the Still Face Experiment and was conducted in 1975 by Dr. Edward Tronick of UMass Boston's Infant-Parent Mental Health Program. The study looked at how a parent's facial reaction can impact an infant's emotional development. Basically mothers looked at their infant's face with an empty and unresponsive expression for two minutes. What the researchers found was that boy infants both reacted with more emotion and were harder to soothe than the female infants.[3]

Now consider another experiment measuring facial responses of men and women to various images. The researchers found that men, like the infant boys, reacted with more immediate emotion when the response was considered "unconscious"; however, when the response time was considered "conscious," they shifted their facial muscles and expression to be less emotionally responsive. Women, on the other hand, were more emotionally responsive when the response was "conscious." The researchers suggested that men have trained themselves to disguise, hide, or mask their emotional expressions.[4]

If you start to weave together this information, it constructs a picture of a man's emotional experience. He responds to emotions at an unconscious level, perhaps to a greater degree than women do; however, he has learned that an emotional response is not as productive for him. On top of that, he is wired to enter into solution mode. This is the emotional highway most often driven by men—they know the way and are comfortable with the route. So, when his partner comes to him emotionally distressed, naturally he feels less competent to handle it in a way that is satisfying to her.

Avrum Weiss, a PhD in psychology who has written extensively about men and women in relationships, says, "Men have all the power in relationships, but don't feel powerful."[5] I think this experience is common for men when it comes to their partner's emotional world. High emotions coming from a partner feel destabilizing for men. They feel their partner's pain immensely, yet they process the emotions differently, likely feeling inadequate and disempowered to handle it well, so they respond in ways that ultimately push their partner away or hurt her. Besides going into solution mode, men will often invalidate the emotion or attempt to minimize the reality of it. Why? Because this intense emotionality stirs up intense emotion in him and threatens his feeling of "providing and protecting" as well as his confidence in the relationship. Furthermore, emotions often feel powerless. Men are socially shaped in a way that tells them they must be powerful. Again, the game feels rigged here.

HIS PERSPECTIVE

I feel like men try to dip into sharing about their perspectives and talking about things that are considered more emotional but then we get feedback like "No better birth control than hearing a man complain." It's like we're only allowed to feel anger. We're trying to change and learn and then society continues to push back.

It just feels like men have zero role models when it comes to being more emotionally invested and vulnerable. I mean, I'll get praise from my wife but it's not really valued explicitly by society or other men. It feels like I'm swimming against the current.

I grew up with a dad that shut down any emotional expression. I was taught not to burden people with my emotional problems and to be self-reliant because no one was really there for me in that way, so I just didn't communicate well. It's been a learning process.

Let me bring this one home. Men want peace because when there isn't peace, they feel responsible for their partner's emotional state. Again, although they feel their partner's emotions intensely, they have been socialized and are "wired" to turn to more logical solutions. Therefore, most men feel less competent in this area of their relationship, plus they don't always understand the need for emotions; sometimes emotions seem like a waste of energy to them. In the section on what women want, one of the areas discussed was emotional attunement. She wants him to be emotionally available, accessible, and adept, yet this is an uncomfortable position for him to occupy, so he minimizes, intellectualizes, or tries to solve it. He feels safer when emotion is at a minimum and peace is abundant.

2. Because if she's emotional, I must be failing.

He is socialized to believe that it's his job to keep her happy and "protect" her. When he can't get this right he feels like he's failing. And then both partners feel dissatisfied.

It's like a cruel joke. We women crave emotional availability, while most men are terrified of our emotionality. We know this all too well, as men have dismissed emotional women as "crazy" since . . . forever. Our needs are often in direct conflict with one another, which is why having insight into our partners can soften our defensiveness and anger and help us step into collaboration.

Weiss asserts in his book that among men, a primary fear surrounding conflict is that it threatens their emotional reassurance in relationships. To summarize, he describes that in Western culture men are expected to leave their mothers for their wives; if they don't, they're called . . . you know it . . . "mama's boys."[6] If you are a mother to a son, I'm sure you'd love for him to maintain a close connection to you throughout your life. Yet if you're married, I bet you hope that your husband won't do this with his own mother. Losing a son to his wife is a painful experience for many mothers, but it is a deep desire of most wives. It's a cruel double-edged sword.

If we analyze this expectation to disconnect from mom, we can begin to understand how the loss of this primary connection and point of emotional safety can create an underlying and deep insecurity in many men. Their later emotional security and reassurance now lies in the hands of their partner. But if their partner isn't satisfied with them, they risk the loss of her emotional reassurance, which creates more feelings of instability. The stakes feel high for her to be okay and not emotional or upset, because it can mean a withdrawal of connection and ultimately rejection.

Furthermore, men have been socialized that their primary role is to provide and protect. If they are not providing a life that offers satisfaction and happiness for their partner and protecting her emotional well-being, it means they're failing. It's an unrealistic standard, but one that men have absorbed deeply into who they are and what their purpose is. If you make a remark about how you wish you had money to do XYZ, you're not just criticizing his ability to care for you, but in many ways you're criticizing him. These socialized constructs feel inseparable from who we are. The same goes for women.

So, when I said at the beginning that both partners want the same end—to be loved and feel secure—this is what I'm talking about. Men feel loved (aka like they're enough and doing a good job) and secure (their partner won't leave them; they won't lose their emotional connection) when there is less fighting, less stress, and less emotionality. When there is peace.

Let me be clear: I'm *not* suggesting one partner stuff all their needs and desires to maintain peace. Not even close. This section is to offer insight so you can work together to have a better relationship, not to suggest one partner has to do the work to cater to the other. We will get into more strategies as to how to do this in later chapters.

Here are some ways to honor his desire for peace:

- Be gentle with your tone and facial expressions. Rolling your eyes and being sarcastic isn't going to go well. Men react with anger when threatened, and this will stir things up and not get you what you want.
- If you've got things you need to discuss with him that you'd like to see changed, set up a time to talk versus letting it trickle out

little by little over time. Give him a moment to prepare for the talk (more on this to come).

- Incorporate expressions of appreciation and words that convey security.
- If he needs a break during a difficult discussion, honor it. This can make a major difference.
- Remember the end goal: Love and security are what he wants too.

Give Him Affection

John Gottman narrows men's complaints in relationships down to two things: (1) too much fighting (which we just covered) and (2) not enough sex. It's stereotypical, but for the most part it applies. I am going to cover sex in more depth in a later chapter, but for now let's focus on the basics of how sex and affection specifically serve an important role in men feeling loved and secure.

A common differentiating question when it comes to sex is this: Do you need sex to feel connected or do you need to feel connected to have sex? For the most part, sex is what helps men feel connected and secure in their relationship.[7] Sex is the reassurance that they're loved and wanted by their partner. I've already reviewed the desire many women have of being pursued by their partner and how the lack of being pursued can feel lonely and like they're invisible and rejected. The same feeling applies to sex for most men.

Furthermore, men are socialized in such a way that their sexual appetite and experiences are directly linked to their masculinity. This is a major reason why men who have low desire have a hard time talking about it with their partners; the shame and embarrassment attached to this issue is too intense for many men to confront. Performance issues are often tied to mental rather than physical problems in that once they experience any issue, they feel inadequate, insecure, and worried it will happen again. Sex and masculinity are inextricably linked and powerful for men and their relationships.

Let me take a minute to address initiation. Initiating sex is an act of vulnerability because it always has a risk of rejection. If you're the one with a higher desire, you've likely felt this sting of rejection from time to time. A common dynamic in relationships is that the partner who initiates more will start to withdraw and stop initiating if rejection occurs too often. This creates distance in the relationship and one partner is ultimately existing without getting some of their needs met.

I want to emphasize that this doesn't mean you have to force yourself to do anything in the sexual relationship. That's not okay and there are all sorts of unhealthy ways of initiating or handling rejection. However, I do want to point out that oftentimes sex is disregarded as a need that isn't very important. After all, there is a difference between a need and a want, and you can live without a want. This is often the mentality of the partner with lower desire. When sex is viewed this way, it suggests it can be cut out of the relationship without causing too much damage. But this isn't the case (unless both partners agree to it). Sex is often, though not always, how men feel reassured, loved, and secure. When this need is minimized, ignored, or criticized it is emasculating and will no doubt create hurt and vulnerability in the relationship. This isn't a popular thing to say, but it needs to be said: Sex is relational, so be careful of categorizing it differently.

Affection extends beyond sex and into the way we touch and speak to each other throughout our relationship. Men are sensitive to criticism; therefore, the way that you speak to each other is important. You may think you're easy on him, or you may recognize that you do tend to speak harshly to him. The way you speak to each other has a powerful impact. It can erode feelings of trust and security in the relationship.

Practical tips for increasing affection in your relationship:

- If you feel safe and good about it in your relationship, initiate sex more. Make him feel wanted.
- Work to increase positive touch when you're together. Hold hands, rub his shoulders, wrap your arms around him for a hug. There is tons of research on the impact of long hugs and reduction of stress.

- Pay attention to how you speak to each other. Do you share criticism more than compliments? In fact, when's the last time you complimented him? Can you incorporate more of this?

Give Him Respect

There are a series of books that discuss the need men have for respect in their relationships, most notably *Love and Respect* by Emerson Eggerichs, PhD. In general, respect means to be esteemed or admired for contributions and achievements. Generally, I'd say both men and women desire respect in their relationships. But I wanted to highlight this one for men because a man's identity and worth are often tied to *what* he does versus *who* he is. This makes respect or lack thereof so much weightier.

If a man's contribution isn't respected it can feel as if *he* isn't valued. If his performance is disrespected, it feels like *he* is disrespected. The dark side of worth being tied to performance is that any criticism of performance becomes deeply personal. In many ways, I hope this encourages empathy toward our male partners. In fact, what it means to be a man is actually a really rigid construct. If you stray too far outside the prescribed norms, you're criticized for not being manly. Fluidity between the masculine and feminine doesn't have the same rules. Men aren't as accepted moving toward the feminine as women are toward the masculine.

In the home, men may be rewarded for more feminine proclivities, but outside the home it's not so welcome. I've often talked with my husband about how the skills necessary for a man to be successful at work directly contradict the skills necessary to be successful in the home. It's a same-rules-don't-apply system. Additionally, what it means to be a man is often really vague. If you asked your partner this, what would he even say? For women our femininity is sort of our essence. We simply are feminine and the ability to give birth gives us this real, tangible outcome that cements what it means to be a woman. For men, it's more ambiguous, which makes their identity in some ways more fragile (unless work has been done here).

This isn't meant to be a condescending statement, but rather insight into what it must be like to be a man. They're taught to rely heavily on themselves, that their worth is performance based, to disconnect from earlier caregivers, to show as little emotion as necessary, to be rational, and that their very existence must be sacrificed in order to provide and protect the ones they love. It seems like a lonely identity. Think about your partner (if you're a man, then think about yourself): When's the last time he had a conversation with another man that wasn't about competition, financials, sports, or hobbies? It rarely happens.

Showing a man respect means that you are aware and sensitive to how you talk to him, how you talk about him in front of others, how you talk about him in his presence in front of others, how you allow him to take the lead on things without micromanaging it, and how you appreciate his contributions to your life and family. Have you ever been on a double date and one of the partners keeps picking on the other, throwing them under the bus or making digs? This behavior cuts deep and will no doubt dramatically impact connection and trust in the relationship.

Here are some practical ways to show respect:

- Offer words of affirmation to your partner. Express appreciation. Notice what he does.
- Brag on him in public.
- Let him get lost sometimes without insisting he stop immediately for directions.

The romantic partner to a man holds a lot of power in the relationship because her approval, admiration, and esteem toward him dramatically impacts how he feels about himself and his good-enoughness. Of course these influences go both ways, because relationships are a dynamic.

get a load of this

Personal Power: Her

- Being as objective as possible, how would you rate your performance in each of the PAR areas? Where could you improve?
- Which expressions of PAR feel easy for you to deliver on? Which ones feel uncomfortable or unclear?
- Which expression does your partner regularly ask for that you feel like you could do better on? Or do you feel unclear in terms of how you actually do it in the way he prefers?
- What stops you or feels like a barrier to hitting PAR in your relationship?

Personal Power: Him

- When you think about PAR (peace, affection, and respect), which one do you feel you need more of in your relationship?
- In what areas do you feel like your partner is doing a good job?
- What are some ideal expressions of peace, affection, and respect for you? If it were caught on camera, consider what each of these three areas would look like from your partner.

Better Together

Talk together about some of the responses you had to these questions. Share two or three things you notice that your partner does for you that hit PAR that you appreciate. Share one or two things you would like more of. Try to be clear when you describe this to your partner.

As you receive your partner's requests, explain back to them what you heard them say and what they're asking for. Offer a couple of ideas of how this change can be implemented in your relationship.

CHAPTER
9

SHARE EXPECTATIONS

where do they come from?

Sharing expectations means hidden ideals are exposed so
that you and your partner can be on the same page and
minimize disappointment.

Almost every relationship encounter has more meaning than appears
on the surface. Sort of like a side mirror on a car, "objects are
closer than they appear," but in this case, "deeper issues are closer to
the surface than you think and will regularly surprise you and sabotage a routine conversation and turn it into something you don't even
recognize anymore." I'm not sure if that would fit well on a mirror,
but you get the idea.

For example, I asked Chad one night as he was doing the dishes
and I was wiping down the counters, "Are you going to do basketball
drills with Effie?"

He responded, "Where do we play? We don't have a driveway
that's meant for this. We don't have a hoop. I may have to join a gym."

"Okay, so why don't you take her to a park or something? Why does this have to be so complicated?" I responded.

"What park? It gets dark so early. When do we even go? What about when I travel?"

I threw my hands up, not even knowing when this started feeling like an argument. "Sure, a gym. Do whatever you think is best. But you're going to play with her, right?"

The question we both should have asked was "Does Effie like basketball?" The answer was no. She ended up playing for two more months and then our basketball days were over.

Little did Chad know—little did I know—that my expectations were shaping my frustrated reaction. In the simplest of explanations, what you need to know about expectations is that they are hopes and ideals (often unspoken), and the further they are from your reality, the greater the disappointment. So let's analyze this encounter.

Here's the behind-the-scenes explanation of this conversation. Chad is logical, methodical, and practical. Like Emmet in *The Lego Movie*, he loves instructions. Give the man a recipe and he will nail it like no other. Make a list and things will be done exactly as it says. However, I am not this way. I am relational, sentimental, and all about the experience (remember the emotional side of the mental load)—the journey, if you will. While usually we complement each other brilliantly, sometimes these differences clash. I was thinking about Effie having something to do that connects her to her dad. He loves basketball, she was learning how to play—what a special time for them. I played too, so I could have jumped in here, but he has a love for the game and is gone so much that I imagined this could become their thing. Also, my dad taught me basketball drills in our Ohio basement; surely Chad could find a place in sunny California to practice?

I was so confused. He rightly was too. The impracticality of playing in a sloped driveway or a grassed backyard just didn't add up in his logical brain. He needed a court and hoop. However, the main drivers of my angst around this topic—actually the whole reason I brought it up—were because I had two main expectations that were driving my desire for Chad to take over basketball training.

1. **Nothing is too big of an inconvenience when it comes to what's important to you.** My dad took me to buy my very first pair of basketball shoes and taught me how to dribble in our Ohio basement. But more memorable to me is that my dad has never—and I mean *never*—let a tiny inconvenience stop him. Sometimes it's annoying in adulthood as it seems like he thinks he can do anything he wants and the answer no doesn't apply. But when you're his kid and it's about making something special happen for you or spending time with you, it's pure magic. He is never inconvenienced by his family, and nothing will stop him from making fun memories happen and making time for us. For some reason, Chad's laundry list of impracticalities felt to me like he was saying that teaching Effie basketball was inconvenient and unimportant to him. This absolutely wasn't the case, but this expectation was operating under the surface, leading to my feelings of frustration and disappointment.

2. **Men should own the domain of sports.** I have a belief, which I didn't really recognize until that very moment, that dads should take the lead on sports. This one is weird. My mom coached all our sports teams. In fact, my dad wasn't that involved in our sports besides attending games and teaching me basketball in the basement. Also, I love sports. I played several and am highly competitive. Taking the lead is something I'd really enjoy doing. But I had an expectation that this was a domain that fell to my husband.

The result of the conversation that night was that I was really irritated with Chad. I'm sure he was with me too. I started to wonder to myself, *Is he just not wanting to take this on? Does he not want to spend time with her? He's making excuses; what's that all about? He must expect me to do this one more thing.* My entire narrative around Chad was affected. It didn't just sour the moment but how I *thought* about him, what I thought I knew about him, and ultimately how I *felt* around him. My feeling of "he's a guy I can just depend on, no matter what" was shaken. I realize this sounds like a minor conversation to have such a major impact, but that's part of the point! It doesn't take much for our expectations to go unmet and ultimately for our image of our partner to be tainted. I'll unpack this process throughout the rest of this chapter, but here's what I'd like you to know about this story.

1. Our expectations of ourselves and how we should show up as a parent and partner will impact the standards we hold about the mental load, what tasks are important, and how well they should be done.
2. Our expectations of our partner and how they should show up as a parent and partner will impact what we expect of them and the standards about the mental load (and so much more) that we hold them to.
3. The distance between our expectations and our reality is the level of disappointment we will feel. The wider the gap, the greater the feelings of falling short we may feel about ourselves or disappointment we may feel about our partners.
4. When our expectations are either met or unmet, we will start to see our partners differently. The way we see them can become more positive or more negative.
5. Ultimately the way we see our partners will influence how connected we feel toward them, how we talk to them, how we treat them, how attractive they are to us, how warm/cold we are toward them, and how we make assumptions about their behavior and words.

Clearly, expectations are important and a major factor in our relationships. But where do they come from?

How Do Expectations Develop?

I liken our expectations to seeds that get planted throughout the course of our lives but that don't actually grow and blossom until the right conditions are in place. These seeds, however, can come from different domains of our lives. Some seeds are planted by our caregivers and others are planted by the messages society sends us.

As the seeds blossom, they develop into storylines we tell ourselves about different people in our lives or aspects of our life. I'm going to help you and your partner explore the storyline you've built around key areas that impact your relationship and the mental load.

There are three sources of information that fuel our expectations: information consumption, societal messaging, and our early experiences. I try to keep things memorable, so if you're flexible with spelling, you can pronounce these as "I see" and it will be easier to recall these areas.

1. Information Consumption

I was listening to a podcast recently and the host and guest were discussing how people don't get their news from legacy media as much as they do from social media and how this has changed politics, especially in the United States. I'd take it further and say it's changed the entire landscape of the information economy. When you look at the number of social media users, it's over half of the world population. Statista estimates around 5.04 billion people (62 percent of the world population) are on social media.[1] Many people are there to just scroll cat content or whatever, but there's an entire social media side that's all about offering "professional advice." At any time you can pick up your phone and find "experts" sharing opinions in fields related to your physical health, your mental health, your skincare routine, what herbs you should be taking, your gut health, your spinal health, your financial health, your dietary health, your parenting approach, your relationships, and on and on it goes.

I know this because I'm part of it. I also know this because I've consumed it. I'm sure we've all had a moment where we watched some piece of content and all of a sudden we were converted to that belief or approach. SOLD! Hook, line, and sinker. The majority of this advice is well-intentioned and it's incredible to be able to have access to so much free information; however, the unfortunate reality is that having more followers doesn't make someone right, truthful, or even helpful. It's just a platform that someone has built and suddenly gained some serious pull and power. I'm pointing this out because these creators start to become authority figures in people's lives, which means they are informing our expectations and standards about various topics.

We also have access to other types of content that show a slew of ideals. I'm sorry but not everyone has a perfectly styled home in varying shades of putty, where the husband cooks dinner every night wearing an apron, and their kids play board games while tastefully dressed in neutrals. It's just fantasyland out there—and it's impactful.

We live at a time where we are bombarded with messages from what we consume all day long. If you don't believe me, look at how much time you've spent on social media over the last week. Now add in TV time, podcast time, book time, and every other source of information and it's dang near constant. This information impacts the expectations we have for ourselves, our kids, our home, our life, and our partners. It fuels comparison culture and can leave us feeling anxious, stressed, overwhelmed, like we're falling short, or just overall terrible about ourselves. Discernment around what we consume is important, because this information infiltrates our mind and colors our standards and expectations.

For the record, this information can be incredibly helpful as well. But being aware of its influence on you is important. Without this awareness, without holding it up to some level of scrutiny and evaluation against your own judgment, values, and personal experience, you're just unknowingly influenced.

2. Societal Messaging

Societal messaging is what we absorb throughout our lifetime from the culture we live in. This messaging can be subtle or more overt, but it's absolutely impactful. Sometimes we aren't even aware of this source of information until we speak to someone who lives or grew up in an entirely different society.

I have a friend from Denmark and she regularly blows my mind with the differences that exist in our two societies. For example, birthday parties. She said she was shocked with the Pinterest party expectation in the United States, which is likely amplified in Southern California, compared to the expectation in Denmark that birthday parties are actually just about family togetherness. She said that the décor and frills of US parties aren't really a priority at all there. Phew—I say we start a no-frills birthday party movement. I mean, how much easier and more enjoyable would that be?

One of the societal messages I somehow picked up along the way was "Dads should be in charge of sports." I'm not really sure where I got that, but there it was creating tension in my conversation with Chad.

The thing to remember about societal messaging is that it shapes the expectations we have about ourselves and others regarding what it means to be a woman, a Christian, a man, an attorney, a good citizen, a good kid, a success, or a failure. Just by existing in whatever society you exist in, you're impacted by this messaging. I liken this to the process of absorbing sunshine and your body making vitamin D. It is happening regardless of whether or not you understand how it happens and even without your awareness of it happening at all.

3. Earlier Experiences

You are impacted by your early experiences. Period. Full stop. No matter your family configuration, it had an impact on you. If you had an absent parent, their absence impacted you. I want to say right away that you do not have to be imprisoned by your early experiences; you have personal power to respond to your experiences in different ways. Specifically, you can repeat, repair, or refuse your early experiences, but ultimately, you have a major say in this!

If you have kids, you likely are invested in being an excellent caregiver. In fact, you may be a hypervigilant caregiver, stressing yourself out trying not to traumatize your kid. The reason why you're feeling this level of commitment and need to parent so well is because you are (along with most other parents of this generation) acutely aware of how much we are affected by our early caregivers and you don't want to mess up your kids. When it comes to how caregivers shape us, we are specifically impacted in certain areas: how we give and receive love, how emotions are expressed, and how we form our identity and expectations of ourselves and others.

My dad has often recalled a memory of his father calling normal things parties. "Ooh, you're eating a banana. I'll eat one, too, and we will have a banana-eating party." Or "Let's do the dishes and have a dishwashing party." My mom, on the other hand, was adopted by a couple who were not very demonstrative, affectionate, or even involved in her life. For example, she was a runner. Her cross-country team won the state championship in Pennsylvania in the seventies and her mother never once attended a race. She has described her childhood as lonely and her accomplishments as largely unacknowledged.

If you combine my mom's and dad's early experiences around celebrations, you've got my dad who had a family that loved celebrations and fun, and my mom who had a family that didn't celebrate much of anything. Previously I mentioned that you have personal power for how you respond to your circumstances. Well, my mom refused to repeat this experience and used her hurt to fuel deep and long-lasting change when she raised my sister and me. My dad just repeated this penchant for parties, and together they made one heck of a celebration-happy couple. It was awesome growing up.

Fast-forward to my married life with Chad. I won't give all the specifics of his growing up experience, but let's just say something major had to have happened for a celebration to occur in his home. Like maybe the pope shows up or someone wins *America's Funniest Home Videos*, I don't know. But celebrations are hard to come by and I've had to pull back in my utter dismay at how little family members are celebrated. This vast discrepancy in early experiences around celebrations created some significant disappointment early on in our relationship. He was shocked when I felt bummed at his lack of celebrating me or something I accomplished, and I was shocked that he was shocked. *How could you not celebrate this?* I never anticipated this being an issue in our relationship when we got married.

Another way early experiences shape our expectations has to do with earlier romantic relationship experiences. Now, earlier could be ten years ago or last week. We are constantly collecting information about our relationships and our partner that leads to making adjustments in how we see them. If you've been cheated on in a past relationship, you may have an expectation of potential hurt or abandonment. If you've asked your partner to take out the trash and it sits in the kitchen for days, your expectations are likely unmet; you'll make an adjustment to how you see your partner, and you will begin to expect your partner to let you down. I'll explain in the next section how expectations shape how we see our partners, but know that all relationship experiences play a role in what you expect in your relationship.

I want you to understand these sources of information that impact your expectations because it will help you to have greater insight into yourself and your partner. If you can recognize that your experiences and the messaging you absorb shape your expectations, you can clearly see how this can lead to major disappointments in your relationship. We then personalize these hurts and accuse our partners of not loving us (or members of our family), but sometimes it's simply different experiences and the troubles associated with combining two people, for life, who come from very different backgrounds.

When I was able to reflect on my expectations for how Chad handled Effie's basketball, I realized many of those expectations came from my childhood experiences and what expectations I had for how a father navigates complications. Chad's reaction created disappointment in me and I felt as if he wasn't loving our daughter the way I thought he should. When I was able to define what was going on with me and my expectations, I was able to communicate with him differently. Specifically, I could present my expectations and say, "Is this what is going on? Because this is the conclusion I'm drawing." He could then contribute his perspective and information to how I was interpreting his behavior, and ultimately we ended up coming up with a solution together. Disappointment resolved and crisis averted.

get a load of this

Personal Power

- What are some expectations that you have that have remained hidden (or unexpressed) but cause disappointment in your relationship?
- Where do these expectations come from?
- When you think about them, do they work for the family and life you and your partner are building together?

Better Together

Each of you think of a time when you had a misunderstanding that was related to expectations. Try to share (without value or judgment attached) the new insight you have around this expectation. Consider where it came from, how it played out in your life, and how you notice it showing up in your relationship with each other.

CHAPTER
10

what story are you telling about your partner?

It would be so great if we simply experienced a little bit of disappointment with an unmet expectation and then everything went back to normal. Unfortunately, that's not how our relationships work. They are dynamic. And unmet expectations can be an event in our relationship that leads to a shift that becomes hard to get out of. It's like the game Mouse Trap when you release one of those marbles and then suddenly all the other pieces are moving and dropping and before you know it, you're stuck, wondering how you got there and why you have such a bad attitude about your partner.

I'm going to share a concept that is really important to understand when it comes to how we get into bad attitudes toward our partners. There are all sorts of ways we can find ourselves in a bad attitude, but feeling like the mental load is unfair, unrecognized, or underappreciated is a fast track to this destination. In turn, feeling like your partner is always complaining about the mental load and criticizing you for what you do or don't do can also lead to a bad attitude. This concept requires some explanation, but it's worth the journey I'm about to take you on, so buckle up.

The idea I'm about to explain is rooted in attachment theory and is called many names (e.g., mental representations), but I'm going to refer to it as a trust picture,* which I'll later simplify to "the story you're telling yourself."

Trust is defined as a feeling of confidence that comes from your belief in someone. As you get to know someone, you sketch a picture of them in your mind. This picture is based on a little bit of what you *factually* know about them but mostly is based on your *opinion and judgments* about what you know. You can think of this picture as a sort of caricature of a person, where some features are exaggerated and others are minimized. Over time, as you keep learning new things about a person, this picture changes. New information is integrated into the picture, and this may shift what you exaggerate or further reinforce it. This picture is always getting reworked, and when you interact with someone almost daily, this picture can change moment-to-moment. Your trust picture operates like a set of glasses or a lens that you look through as you see your partner (or anyone else for that matter, since you have pictures for everyone).

Your trust picture impacts how you

- interact with others,
- interpret the words and behavior of others,
- develop judgments about others, and
- predict behavior, reactions, and opinions of others.

Now, this is the part that stings. You are entirely in charge of how you sketch your trust picture of others and yourself. Why? Well, in part because you are the one who decides what to exaggerate and what to

---

* A trust picture comes from John Van Epp, as featured in his courses Couple LINKS and Rock Solid Marriage and book *Better Together*.

minimize. You decide where you place your focus. You are also the one who has a unique set of judgments and opinions that come from . . . yup, you guessed it: information consumption, societal messaging, and earlier experiences. As much as we hate to admit this, there are tons of different interpretations for any given experience, and these interpretations are largely based on your own expectations shaped by those three different sources we talked about in the last chapter.

HER PERSPECTIVE

The mental load really changes how I see my partner, and it is definitely more negative than it used to be.

The mental load impacts how I view him in nearly every situation.

Let me give you an example.

Partner A: Gets up in the morning and gets the kids ready for school. She encourages her partner to take the morning off, so she makes breakfast, takes care of the dog, and then drops the kids off for the day.

Partner B: Gets up in the morning and enjoys the breakfast made by his partner and then heads out of the house to take a bike ride.

Partner A: Comes home from dropping the kids at school and finds the sink full of dirty dishes from the morning and Partner B showered and dressed on the couch scrolling social media.

I would bet that you've lived this scenario before. You also may need to take a small break because you're so outraged reading this that you just need a moment. Take all the time you need.

Now, I'm going to analyze this scenario without saying one partner is right or wrong. Instead I'm going to show you how your expectations and trust picture work in your relationship. Keep this in mind: I'm not going to make a judgment about what happened; I'll just talk through it objectively as an example.

Partner A

Expectations. If Partner A is bothered by coming home to a sink full of dishes, it's most likely because of the following:

- She has the expectation of *when* the mess should be cleaned up and that taking care of things around the home *should* be done before resting and leisure. She likely operates this way. Others first, then her.
- She has an expectation that the house is relatively tidy. Not over-kill, but you definitely clean up the dishes after breakfast.
- She has the expectation that he would appreciate all that she did in the morning (that he didn't have to do) and would show his appreciation and care for her by cleaning up the mess. This also implies that he doesn't care for her or appreciate her if he didn't take care of the mess.

Trust picture. Now let's sketch this trust picture based on her having the above expectations.

Partner A walks in and sees the mess. She anticipated that it would be cleaned up, and sure enough, here it is looking her square in the face. Her internal dialogue sounds like *What's new, me taking care of everyone and everything? How was that bike ride, fella? You enjoy yourself? I bet that hot shower felt nice as I'm still walking around in my yoga pants, not even dressed yet. I probably won't even be able to get dressed today. Must be nice having absolutely no feelings of responsibility for anyone but* you.

In a flash, her trust picture shifted to a very negative place by just the sight of those dishes alone. Likely, she's experienced a similar scenario with her partner in the past, so all those previous moments that fit this storyline are conjured up in her head. She's now looking over at the King of the Castle perched on his sectional-shaped throne, wielding his electronic scepter. *Who the heck does he think he is?!* Her trust picture is now really negative, highlighting all the ways that he fits this description. If she starts doing the dishes, I bet she does them loudly.

Her entire presence has shifted to tense and irritated. Underneath it she feels unappreciated, and I assure you, she's not feeling too into him. If he strode over to her and put the moves on—"Hey, babe, the kids are at school, so why don't we . . . you know"—no doubt she'd be disgusted and *not* in the mood.

Do you see how her expectations and interpretation of what happened has an immense power over how she sees her partner and feels about him? Do you see how easy it is to assume how her partner feels and thinks about her and the situation and how these assumptions can lead to hurt and misunderstanding?

Now let's check in with Partner B.

Partner B

Partner B is chilling out on the couch. He had a great morning and is coming off a long travel stretch. He's happy to be home and is feeling relaxed. He's excited to hang with his partner when she gets home from drop-off.

Expectations. If he is caught off guard by her tension, it's likely because of the following:

- He has an expectation that he can take care of himself before doing anything around the house. Him first, others next. What's the harm?
- He has the expectation that "morning off" extends to all things.
- He has a lower expectation of what clean and tidy looks like and doesn't feel guilty if things aren't perfect.
- He has an expectation that his partner will be easygoing when she gets home—after all, she said to "take the morning off" and that they can hang together for the day just chilling out while the kids are at school.
- He maybe even expects to get some action when she gets home; after all, he's feeling pretty good.

Trust picture. Now let's sketch his trust picture.

Partner A walks into the house and he glances over his shoulder and sees her tense up. He calls, "Hey, how'd it go?" from the couch and she curtly replies, "Fine," as she stands at the kitchen sink. He furrows his brow: *What's her deal?* His internal dialogue may sound like *I can't tell what's going on with her. I thought she was going to be excited to hang out with me; she was fine when she left and now she seems irritated. Did I do something?* He scans his recollection of the morning. Nope, nothing. He lifts his head up. "Are you okay?"

"Yup, fine," she retorts. Okay, something doesn't add up. He had sketched a picture of her earlier where he was focusing on how she was being generous and giving him time to take care of himself, but now this doesn't fit; she seems bothered. His picture starts to focus on the parts of her that come across as uptight, anxious, and short with him. *Gosh, why does she seem stressed out all the time? I don't get it.* The "she's uptight and stressed" lens clicks into view for him and he gets up and leaves the room. He's worried her emotionality will come out at him and he is creating as much distance as possible. *I guess we're not getting in an early afternoon session like I thought we would. What's new?*

His trust picture of her shifted from grateful—although it doesn't sound like he expressed it—to fearful of her "wrath." He distanced himself in order to avoid confrontation with her and was confused about why she was upset. Likely, his avoidance just added fuel to the fire. On top of all of this, even though he never spoke it out loud, he was hoping to have sex with her. So when she arrived home and her mood changed, he felt a pang of rejection. His expectations were distant from his reality, and so disappointment likely resulted.

You could easily see how this couple could go round and round getting deeper into this dynamic. He feels rejection, she feels disappointment, which kills her desire, and both feel hurt and don't really have a clear understanding of each other's perspectives. It wouldn't take much for their trust pictures to be sketched in the most negative light and for their attitudes toward each other to become sour. At this point, if this couple didn't reset in some major way, either together or on their own, this small incident could set off a pattern of interactions between the two of them that quickly erodes connection and feelings of love.

In short, the trust picture is "the story I'm telling myself about _____." The story Partner A told herself about her partner was that he was entitled and didn't care about her and appreciate her or else he would have cleaned the dishes. The story Partner B told himself about his partner was that she was often uptight and grumpy, and that she was rarely "in the mood."

Remember, a trust picture is based on a degree of factual knowledge—in this case, the dishes didn't get done—but more so on the opinions and judgments about the knowledge. These judgments are often influenced by the three sources we discussed earlier (information consumption, societal messaging, and earlier experiences). There is an interaction between your expectations and what you know about your partner that feeds into your trust picture. If what you know falls short of your expectations, you're likely going to be disappointed. If you get to know something about your partner and it challenges your expectations, you may adjust them. We will explore this later, but you have options for reshaping both your expectations as well as your trust picture toward your partner. Both can have a positive influence on your relationship.

Stories That Sabotage

Before we get into solutions, I want to call out a common tendency when it comes to the mental load, which is that we sometimes tell ourselves stories that sabotage our ability to hand things off and renegotiate the mental load and stories that even sabotage our partner's initiative taking. As we write the story we're telling ourselves about our partner, we are regularly making adjustments based on our past experiences with them and based on information consumption, societal messaging, and earlier experiences.

I say this to reassure you that your story isn't pure fiction, but rather it's written out based on your real experiences as well as your interpretation of these experiences. However, because you're the author of this story, it can start to become saturated with negativity when you focus on certain qualities of your partner and you start moving negative aspects to the foreground and the more positive ones to the background. You create the storyline, you create the character of your partner in the story, you are the one that is deciding what their motives are, and you are making meaning of their actions. It's all in your hands. And when our storyline becomes overly negative, we start to write stories that sabotage.

Let me give you some examples of common statements that indicate you're writing stories that sabotage:

- I shouldn't have to ask!
- If I don't do it, no one will.
- It's just easier to do it myself than explain it to my partner.
- No matter what I do, I don't get it right, so why even try?
- Her standards are way too high; this is on her.
- It's never enough; doing this one little thing won't even matter to her, so what's the point?

The problem with these stories is that they impact behavior. If you believe that you shouldn't have to ask, you won't. And then your partner won't know.

If your story says, "No matter what I do, I don't get it right, so why even try?" you will likely cop out of taking initiative in your relationship around the mental load. If your story is "If I don't do it, no one will," I bet you walk around the house huffing and puffing while doing all the things and resenting your family when they don't "know" that they're supposed to jump in and relieve you. These stories are all too easy to tell, but they don't move you forward when it comes to finding a better distribution of the mental load.

The next chapter will walk you through how to navigate expectations in your relationship so that you can see each other's perspective and avoid having a bad attitude toward each other that eventually erodes connection. You will be guided through three steps for dealing with expectations: reflect, revise, and reinforce. Let's get to it.

get a load of this

Personal Power

- What is a reoccurring storyline you tell yourself about your partner? How does this impact how you feel toward them? Respond to them? Treat them?
- What stories that sabotage do you tell yourself that end up getting in the way of handing off more of the mental load or taking more of it on?

Better Together

Talk about how you will check your storylines with each other when you're making assumptions or drawing negative conclusions. What's your plan for fact-checking in the moment?

CHAPTER

11

SHARE EXPECTATIONS

reflect, revise, reinforce

When it comes to sharing expectations and seeing each other in a positive light, there are three steps. These steps will help your relationship tremendously in a broad sense and specifically around the mental load. I will use examples as applications through the chapter to help you and your partner navigate your expectations around the mental load. Let's explore these three steps:

1. Reflect on your expectations.
2. Revise your expectations and your story.
3. Reinforce your new story so that you can see your partner in a better light.

1. Reflect on Your Expectations

Earlier I mentioned that expectations are planted like seeds throughout our entire lives and when the right conditions present, they blossom. This sprinkling of sunshine and water on these dormant seeds happens at two pivotal times in one's relationship life:

1. when you transition from dating to married (or in a long-term committed relationship)
2. when you transition from partners to parents

There are, of course, other times, but these tend to be the most jarring and applicable to the topic of the mental load. What happens is that a lifetime of developing expectations suddenly rises to the surface and colors your perspective of your partner. It really is shocking for many couples.

During the first transition you no longer see your partner as your boyfriend (or whatever term you used) but rather as your husband or permanent partner, and the same goes for your girlfriend becoming your wife. With these terms comes a whole different set of expectations that click into view, like that big device they use to check your eyes at the eye doctor's office. Does A or B look better? How about now? The flipping of the lens from dating partner to spouse is significant because with it brings all of the things you've learned throughout the years about what it means to be a partner and what you'll expect from your partner. For example, if you came from rather traditional parents but you see yourself as more progressive, don't be all that surprised if after you say "I do" you start to notice some of your parents' dynamics playing out in your own relationship. The lens has shifted and if you don't have insight into why you act the way you do or think the way you do, that default takes over without your awareness.

The second huge transition is partner to parent, and this is yet another flipping of the lens, which brings with it all the expectations you've garnered over the years about what a good parent does and looks like. You likely aren't even aware of these but they play out in your relationship, causing tensions and disgruntlement.

As you work through this next section, remember that everyone is different. Some people will look at these statements and just know right away what their answers are. Others will have to really think these through. Do whatever works best for you in whatever season of life you're in. I'm going to try to make this as simple as possible so that you don't have to think so hard. I'll give you categories of expectations, but feel free to add things if I missed them.

Explore each of these statements on your own and/or with your partner:

Expectations for self	
The expectations I have for myself as a PARTNER are	
The expectations I have for myself as a PARENT are	
The expectations I have for myself as a PARTNER AFTER becoming a parent are	
Expectations for partner	
The expectations I have for my partner as a PARTNER to me are	
The expectations I have for my partner as a PARENT are	
The expectations I have for my partner as a PARTNER AFTER becoming a parent are	

Next use the broad categories of expectations on the next page to help you complete the above statements. These are here to help you come up with ideas, so don't feel like you have to rigidly stick to these—they're just offerings. You can also use the Additional Resources QR code to print out a blank Expectations Worksheet to fill in.

I just want to acknowledge for a moment that thinking in this way isn't typical, but I know this will help you, which is why I tried to give you examples and categories so that you're able to work through this exercise effectively but without pulling a hammy.

Identifying your expectations is one of the most important steps because, for the most part, they live in the dark. Expectations are the projected hopes and ideals, which often are unspoken, that have a way of creeping into our relationships, so when you can unearth these it gives you the opportunity to relate to them in a new way, both as an individual

		DEFINITION	EXAMPLE TOWARD SELF	EXAMPLE TOWARD PARTNER
Area of expectations	ATTITUDE	One's general disposition. Is it cheery? Positive? Agreeable?	I will exude patience and pleasantness in parenthood.	My partner won't complain and will be happy most of the time.
	APTITUDE	The competence and mastery one possesses in life, at home, and in parenthood.	I know I will have a finely tuned intuition in parenthood.	My partner will know how to take care of the kids just like I do.
	APPEARANCE	What you think you'll look like; this includes your appearance or even the appearance of your space.	My home will be spotless. Pinterest-worthy most of the time.	My partner will be put together and take care of themselves.
	ACTIVITY	How you imagine spending your time and the amount of energy you will have.	I will have the energy to enroll the kids in tons of extracurriculars.	My partner will be engaged in the kids' extracurriculars just like I am.
	AFFECTION	How you imagine the level of warmth and affection in your relationship.	I will be loving in words and actions in my relationship.	My partner and I will have an active sex life.
	AVAILABILITY	How you imagine the emotional and physical availability.	I will be emotionally open and available to my partner.	My partner will be there for me no matter what.

and as partners. Once you've identified them, you are empowered to do something about them. You get to choose to relate to your expectations differently. This may mean that you, as an individual, adjust your expectations or that you, as a couple, negotiate them differently.

I am going to guide you through some questions to explore by yourself and/or with your partner to get clearer on your expectations. These structured questions can be helpful because it is often difficult to decipher when an expectation is actually too extreme. Our expectations are subjective, after all, and so what's extreme to one person may not be extreme to the other. Stop trying to prove to your partner that their expectations are ridiculous and instead start listening to their heart and what's important to them. Think about the history and experiences underneath the expectation. Does the expectation make more sense now? The goal is for both of you to feel like you are respected and honored in your relationship, and the most effective way of getting to this place is to listen to and validate each other's perspectives and genuinely care about making changes that benefit the relationship.

One final note: Going through these questions may feel mechanical if you do them with your partner. It may feel like you're in a business meeting or that this is just way too awkward and formal. I'm going to shoot you straight: Get over your bad self. If this is causing you difficulties in your relationship, then you have to learn a new way of existing. And doing things differently takes time. Much like learning a new sport, you'll likely step up to the plate and swing that bat over and over until you master your mechanics. New skills take practice—over and over again until they become second nature. The same applies in relationships. Yes, it's mechanical, because it's helping you think through something in an entirely new way.

Explore Your Expectations Exercise

1. What is your expectation?
2. On a scale of 1 to 10, 1 being "Not at all" and 10 being "Very," how important is this expectation to you?
3. What does this expectation mean to you? What's the backstory?
4. On a scale of 1 to 10, how important is this expectation to the functioning of your home, family, or relationship?
5. What is your revised expectation?
6. What's your plan for when the old expectation shows up in your relationship?

I want you to think about how these expectations shape the story you tell yourself about yourself and your partner. As I explained earlier, this story has a major influence on the way that you see yourself and your partner, how you treat them, your attitude toward them, and how you actually behave in your relationship. You may be telling yourself a story about how you're always doing everything for everyone else and your partner doesn't care about you, that your partner just sees you as the hired help. If this is your story, how does this impact your relationship? Consider your relationship storyline and the character each of you plays. I'll get you started.

Considering the characters my partner and I each play, what story am I telling myself about

- myself as a parent and partner?
- my partner as a parent and partner?

Now that you've identified your expectations in your relationship as well as the story you're telling yourself, you can make some changes.

2. Revise Your Expectations and Your Story

When it comes to making these changes around expectations, you have three primary options. Please know that your resolution may require more than one of these options or even that you do one option and your partner does another. Here are the three ways of handling expectations:

1. **Lighten up:** This means you can adjust the expectations by lowering them or compromising with your partner to find a better middle ground.
2. **Let it go:** This means that you can just ditch the expectation entirely. Perhaps you have an expectation of your home being perfectly put together all the time, yet you're spending every waking hour tidying the house. You're grumpy when the kids pull the Legos out for the hundredth time because you "just cleaned them up." Maybe this expectation is causing you way more hassle and grief than necessary, so you ditch it entirely.
3. **Level up:** This means that either you or your partner steps up

to meet the expectation. When it came to celebrations, Chad leveled up his game. He realized that celebrations were sort of engrained in my head and heart more deeply than "not celebrating" was for him. We also decided that we wanted our kids to experience being celebrated, so this became an expectation he leveled up to for me but also for our kids.

Please note that you can incorporate any combination of these options as you start to move through different expectations that have caused you difficulty in your relationship or in how you view yourself or your partner.

Let's go back to the dishes story from the last chapter and consider an example of how Partner A could rework one of her expectations in each of the three ways.

Expectation: She has the expectation of *when* the mess should be cleaned up and that taking care of things around the home *should* be done before resting and leisure. She likely operates this way. Others first, then her.

1. **Lighten up:** She recognizes that this expectation of others first and then self means that she regularly is frustrated when her partner doesn't operate by the same standard *and* it means she is regularly sacrificing her own needs and rest. Overall, it leads to resentment. She decides to have more flexibility around this expectation and be more intentional around deciding when she will put herself first and let the dishes sit.

2. **Let it go:** She decides that her preference of timing doesn't need to reign supreme. She would love for him to have done the dishes before relaxing, but she knows that if she doesn't do them first, he will most likely get to it later. She decides to ditch the expectation entirely. She also recognizes that she told him to take the morning off, so maybe his interpretation of this was different from hers.

3. **Level up:** This expectation feels like a nonnegotiable for her. Part of why she's upset is that it's happened too many times that

he just sits and doesn't help out and she ends up angry and hurt. She wants him to level up. She initiates a conversation around the expectation with him in an effort to renegotiate it together.

Now, I can already hear the protests: "But her expectations are too extreme" or "I will be the one compromising on all of my expectations until we just live in a pigsty." When one partner is repeatedly compromising their expectations and the other partner refuses or regularly accuses them of having expectations that are too high, resentment will almost always result. Why? Because it feels unfair and invalidating. Remember, you're in a relationship that consists of two people, not a relationship where one person is the authority on all things without considering the other person.

Oftentimes in relationships, both partners will be required to do some revising of their expectations. Be open to seeing things a new way and remember that there is often a historical influence or deeper value attached to these expectations. When you discuss them with openness, a team mentality, and a commitment to fostering closeness and connection, you will not find these expectations so disruptive or irritating.

Another regular revision that couples almost always need to add to their repertoire is revising the story they're telling themselves about their partner. This practice of editing and rewriting the storyline will help to keep you and your partner from falling into chronically bad attitudes toward each other.

Let's review how impactful your trust picture, or the story you're telling yourself, is using the dishes example from earlier. This time we will analyze Partner B. This analysis will give you a clear example of how powerful your trust picture is in your relationship.

Trust picture principles	If he sees his partner as uptight and stressed out	If he sees his partner as needing care
Begins with what you know factually	Partner B sees the mood of his partner shift when she returns home from school drop-off.	Partner B sees the mood of his partner shift when she returns home from school drop-off.

Is influenced by what you focus on and judgments/ opinions about what you know	He focuses on how she regularly becomes stressed out and uptight. *She told me to take the morning off, so why is she acting this way? Just more of the same.*	He focuses on gratitude for all she did for him and concern for her well-being. If she's acting stressed, something must be wrong.
Shapes your attitude toward yourself and others	He is disappointed and a little irritated she doesn't seem lighter and happier. He feels hurt and rejected and confused by her reaction.	He feels compassion, empathy, and curiosity.
Becomes the lens that impacts your predictions, interpretations, assumptions, and behavior	He leaves the room, distancing himself from her to avoid her emotionality. He doesn't feel like getting in trouble when he doesn't even understand what he did wrong.	He approaches her and asks her what's wrong and what he can do.
Is something you are in charge of and responsible for	He is entirely in charge of his interpretation and where he puts his focus: He puts it on her tension.	He is entirely in charge of his interpretation and where he puts his focus: He puts it on her need for care.

In order to maintain a relationship that doesn't regularly exist in a place of bad attitudes, you have to reset your story. You have to start over, clean it out, and shift your focus onto the ways that your partner makes your life better.

Following is an exercise that will help you rewrite your story. The first step is to shift your focus onto the ways your partner makes your life better. You may need to make some shifts in how you see yourself too. While the practice of shifting your story may feel mechanical or pained at first, this is a practice you should engage in regularly. It requires intentional effort to make these revisions, but if you remember that your attitude can change quickly toward your partner, you can clearly see how necessary it is to routinely recalibrate how you perceive your partner and the storyline you've created. When you've got this down, it only takes a few minutes, and you can do it anywhere because it's done all in your head.

	The story I'm telling myself about . . .	My focus is currently on . . .	If I shifted my focus to more positive qualities, I'd focus on . . .
Myself as a parent and partner			
My partner as a parent and partner			

While you are in charge of how you tell the story about your partner, there are times when you may need more information. Especially in those times when you feel like you've been gracious and patient yet nothing is changing or you are having a hard time seeing it any other way.

Following are prompts you can use to explore a conversation with your partner about how to uncover and better understand your attitude toward them. However, please know that one of the most helpful strategies is to fact-check your story and ask questions in the moment. When you feel that storyline pushing its way to the forefront of your mind, be a fact-checker and take a moment to run it by your partner and allow them to add to the story. An example would sound like this: "Hey, just checking, are you feeling bothered by what I said or is something else going on? I didn't want to assume without running it by you." We all know the danger of making assumptions, so do your best not to be a donkey and check them out in the moment.

Here are some conversation starters you can use to involve your partner in editing the story you're telling yourself.

- I've felt bothered by something lately. Would now be a good time to talk it through with you?
- The story I've been telling myself about why you do _____ is _____. Is this accurate? Can you help me revise this?

- I always try to see you in the best light. But I want you to know that when you respond to me in that way, it feels really invalidating and that makes it really hard for me to keep a good attitude toward you.
- When I come to you with a need I have and you get defensive, it's hard for me not to interpret that as you not caring about my need. I've been doing mental gymnastics to see you in a good light but something has to give here.
- I realize that my attitude has been off toward you lately. I would like to share it with you because I can't adjust it without your input. Can you handle this now? Or when is a good time?
- You haven't done anything wrong, but I am feeling like _____ is really unfair. It's impacting how I feel toward you. I need to talk this out with you. I realize it's me holding on to this frustration.

These two skills—reflecting on your expectations and regularly revising the story you tell yourself about your partner—will dramatically change your relationship. I am not speaking in hyperbole; if you do these two things, you will have a new relationship. Unclear expectations and overly negative storylines sabotage relationships all the time and rot them from the inside out, which can sour the tone and lead to hardened hearts and loveless relationships. You have so much power in these two tools to make a difference. I can't wait to see what you do with them.

3. Reinforce Your New Story

Getting into the habit of reinforcing your new story will take time, but each time you do it, you will become better at it. Practice reinforces change. Practice will help this become second nature.

Whatever story you tend to tell yourself about your partner becomes the lens that you see them through. If you focus on all the ways they let you down, reject you, or criticize you, it is all that you will see. You will begin to anticipate this behavior and treat them as if they've done these things, even when they haven't. You will assume bad intent and this will color the way you treat them. But when you tell yourself a different story, you can start to see your partner in a new light.

For example, Chad has this tendency to take his socks off and leave them in balls around the house. The story I could tell myself about this is that he thinks I'm his maid. He is entitled and doesn't care about how I like to keep our home tidy. This story is completely in my hands. Here's the thing: Chad travels nearly every week for work. He's rarely home and, overall, he's a really clean guy. He appreciates and loves me. So, I tell myself another story and it goes like this: Those balled up black socks are a reminder that my husband is home with me. He isn't disrespecting me; he feels comfortable in our home and I want that. I don't want him walking around on eggshells, and I certainly don't want to live that way either.

This tiny little graciousness I offer him makes a massive difference in my attitude toward him and our relationship. There is a key piece to all of this, and it's that *you are the author*. You are in charge of how you write the story and where you place your focus. A simple rule of thumb when it comes to crafting your story is that *gracious inter-pretations lead to good interactions*. The more you offer each other generous and gracious storylines and interpretations of behaviors and experiences, the more positive your interactions will be.

If you gain nothing from this book but learning how to regularly rewrite your story about your partner, you will have an infinitely bet-ter relationship. This tendency to focus on the ways our partners let us down and then use that focus to interpret their motives and assume meaning from their behaviors has the potential to create grooves in our relationship that we and our partners just can't seem to step out of. It's easy to then justify almost any discourtesy toward them. This is a very slippery slope. Learn how to regularly shift your focus toward the qualities you appreciate about your partner, offer gracious interpre-tations of their motives, and try to see them in the best light possible.

Friends, you've made it! This chapter can change your relationship forever if you work to excavate your expectations and rewrite your story of each other regularly.

get a load of this

Personal Power

- Identify one storyline about your partner that needs revising. Change where you focus and consider that there are other sides to this storyline that likely bless your life. Intentionally make this shift to revise your story.
- Commit to checking in on your storyline regularly so that you can make revisions as needed.

Better Together

- Discuss your expectations in your relationship and/or around the mental load. Brainstorm ways you could lighten up, let it go, or level up.
- Determine a plan for "in the moment" when you notice your storyline toward your partner is becoming overly negative. Normalize fact-checking each other and discuss what this can look like in real time. Have a plan, folks!

CHAPTER
12

it's all about initiative

Sharing ownership means that you both feel and act on a sense of responsibility for the well-being of your home and family life.

Chad and I have a dog named Teddy, short for Theodore Roosevelt. Somewhere along the way, my family started naming dogs after political figures. (I've had a Lincoln and our family dog was Benjamin Franklin.) Chad gave Teddy to me as a gift on our first Christmas as a married couple. He's a mix of Brussels griffon (the dog from *As Good as It Gets* . . . also, I really aged myself) and a bichon. He packs a whole lot of smarts and stench in his ten adorable pounds.

At the time of writing this, he's almost sixteen years old and requires very little in terms of care. He can hold his pee for an absurd length of time, and besides my cooking for him (he's got allergies, which is a game changer), he doesn't need much. In the busyness of our lives, his low-maintenance quality can make him easy to forget. Chad and I never officially discussed who handles Teddy's care, because we typically just volley it pretty effortlessly. Chad gets up early to feed him and gives him his meds, I cook for him, Chad usually walks him, we both let him out, and so on.

However, on one unusually busy baseball tournament weekend, we left the house armed with our cooler and bleacher seats with no plan in place for Teddy. In fact, I don't think either of us even remembered to consider a plan. In full transparency, usually Chad will remind me to ask my parents to let him out, but this time he didn't. Many games . . . too many games later, I audibly gasped *Home Alone*–style (Teeeeddy) remembering our poor little pooch, who had been alone all day and was likely up to his eyeballs in pee. I frantically texted my parents, then called, and embarrassingly admitted we forgot to consider our little guy. Thankfully, all was well, and my parents found him sleeping in his bed, no messes to be found.

But the takeaway of this story is that Chad and I never really discussed who had ownership over Teddy's care. When ownership isn't clear, things fall between the cracks, balls get dropped, and dogs get left for hours while you eat peanuts and stress about your kid's at bat. When there isn't clarity around who is in charge of what, responsibility gets diffused and this leaves loads of opportunity for miscommunication and arguments. Ownership requires information and knowledge of the home and family life. A sense of ownership facilitates initiative taking, the gold standard for navigating the mental load.

Taking Initiative

In my survey of women about the mental load, when they were asked what they needed the most when it comes to the mental load, 50 percent responded, "My partner to take more initiative." This was, by far, the most popular response. If we are being totally honest, we want clones. We want Dolly-the-sheep-esque cute little clones of ourselves walking around the house intuiting exactly what needs to be done, when it needs to be done, and how it should be done. Alas, this is not a possibility . . . yet (dah dah daaaaa). And so, for the most part, women have come to terms with the reality that their partners may not "see" all that they see.

Most women respond by lowering their expectations, sucking it up, stuffing it down, and getting less of what they need. The typical outcome of this practice is to cruise along for a while feeling decent about carrying the majority of the mental load, but then something gets added to her plate or she enters a busier season of life and all of a sudden it rushes to the surface, bubbling over. She's stressed and bothered again. Or she may carry it, appearing to have it all together, but then she's never really got the energy or headspace to engage in much of a sexual relationship. And no doubt other areas of her life, most often herself, take a major hit. She seems fine, but really she's at max capacity.

Eve Rodsky coined the ingenious term *she*-fault partner in her book *Fair Play*, referencing the tendency for all the things to default to women in relationships. I spoke about this earlier in chapter 4. The outcome of this, however, is that like it or not, women are then the owners of all the things *until* the things are delegated. This puts her in the position of being the coach of the relationship, calling all the plays on the home front. Some women enjoy being in charge of these things, but even if they do, most women will hit a place of overwhelm, and in that instant it becomes too much.

The thought of delegating something in the moment *and* explaining it all to their partner just adds to their current overwhelm. Many times, she won't explain it and she'll do it herself because in the short term this just feels easier. This moment likely includes huffing and puffing and banging around, her wondering why she's the only one who can see everything that needs to be done. The problem is that this tipping point into overwhelm, without the capacity to explain and delegate, just means that she will continue to carry the bulk of the mental load on her own. It may be an "easier" solution in the short term, but it has a long-term negative effect, perpetuating the dynamic that already exists. So nothing actually changes; it's a vicious cycle.

The goal is for both you and your partner to feel a sense of joint ownership over home and family life. When you both feel a sense of ownership, versus her owning it all and then dishing it out to you, it helps her feel like she has a partner who is reliable, is there for her, and is invested and cares about her and the family.

Sharing ownership also means that she doesn't feel like she has to occupy the place of the family nag, doing the reminding, and the telling, and the following up. This helps her relax more in the relationship and in life. This also helps her partner to feel less like he's living with someone who is stressed out and overwhelmed. That intensity can be difficult to be around, and no doubt it doesn't feel good to her either because it really stinks to feel like you've become the drill sergeant of the home. There's more warmth, connection, sex, and teamwork when both partners share ownership.

The goal when sharing ownership is this: that both partners feel and act on a sense of responsibility for the well-being of the home and family life. But what if your partner is resistant and doesn't want to take ownership of the mental load?

When Your Partner Is Resistant

Okay, here's where it gets sticky. I am cycling through all the conversations I've had with people about where their partners fall on this continuum, and I know that some of you reading this book have a partner who is resistant. Here's what you need to know: The level of confrontation around the mental load is directly related to their willingness to participate. Look at the following figure.

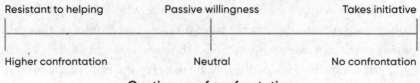

Continuum of participation

Resistant to helping	Passive willingness	Takes initiative
Higher confrontation	Neutral	No confrontation

Continuum of confrontation

Having these confrontational conversations is deeply uncomfortable. Unfortunately, if you feel this resistance, you aren't alone. Here are the responses from my survey data of women when asked, "When you talk about the mental load, what happens?"

- 61 percent responded, "I'm told, 'Well, just tell me what to do.'"
- 53 percent said, "It just turns into a competition of who does what or who does more."
- 52 percent said, "My partner gets defensive."
- 48 percent said, "My partner just doesn't understand the concept of the mental load."
- 37 percent said, "My partner tells me to just not do so much."
- 19 percent said, "I have just given up."

I provided you with some troubleshooting techniques in chapter 4 for defensiveness and issues around mindset, so I want to offer some suggestions as to how to respond to resistance in your relationship. But don't forget you can refer back to those suggestions as well. I recognize that some of these may sound condescending, but that's not the intention; your tone and delivery will matter. I also want to say, these are going to be more confrontational examples, because this is assuming you've tried having the conversation more than once and it continues to get derailed. This isn't a first-attempt approach, and the tone will be more direct and combative than a first-time conversation. Here are some approaches to confronting a resistant partner.

1. **Peel the onion.** I think of this approach as reflecting back questions that remove, layer by layer, their rationale for resistance or require them to think through the cause and effect of what they're saying. You are trying to help them articulate their *why* and clarify their intention. Here are some examples: "How are you wanting me to feel when you say that?" "What are you wanting me to take from what you just said?" "What is the point you're getting at?" One specific to the mental load may sound like this: "So you're wanting me to hear from you that you refuse to participate around the house?"

2. **Communicate relationship goals.** Requiring your partner to reflect on and communicate their goals for your relationship often highlights the incongruencies between their actions and desired outcome. If you want closeness yet you don't show up for each other, you won't have closeness. If you want more sex yet you dump the entire workload on your partner, taking them for granted, chances are it's not happening. You're hoping, through the conversation, to help your partner move toward a willingness to change. Here are some phrases you can incorporate to ask about your partner's relationship goals:
   » If our relationship was "perfect," what would be different? (FYI: The response may be something like "You'd just be happy." The follow-up could be something like "What are you willing to do to get to that place?")
   » What do you want for our life together?
   » How do you want our relationship to *feel*? Or how do you want to *feel* in our relationship?

3. **Call out unilateral decision making.** It can be helpful to point out that resistance to engage in family and home involvement is a unilateral decision that dramatically impacts your quality of

life. If this is how your relationship functions, does this same "right" apply to you? Does your partner not want to have a relationship where both people feel valued?

4. **Avoid assumption of intent.** We explored this in the last chapter when I gave prompts for discussing your attitude toward your partner. But when a partner is resistant, there comes a point when it's hard to draw any other conclusion than that they don't care about you or your well-being. This is a vulnerable place for your relationship, and calling this out to your partner can be helpful. Be careful of sounding like you're issuing a threat, which can increase defensiveness. It's helpful to use "I statements" and "feel statements" versus stating things as though they're a fact or suggesting you are absolutely sure of your partner's intention. It may sound like this: "When I come to you hurting and struggling and you just continue to argue with me, it feels like you don't care about me. It feels like you'd rather win or not participate around the house than show up for me as a partner. I am not sure how you want me to feel when you say these things."

5. **Disengage from the power struggle.** When you continue to butt heads over an issue with your partner or they are locked into their position and perspective, it can be helpful to simply step out of the power struggle. Imagine playing tug-of-war and just letting go of the rope. When you do this with your partner in a conversation it sounds something like this: "I can tell you're really set on not changing how we handle the mental load together. I've tried and I'm not getting anywhere. I'm stepping away from this conversation, but I have to be transparent with you. Holding tight to your perspective has repercussions for me, like always feeling tense and stressed and not having a lot of desire, and my attitude toward you shifts because I didn't realize this is what I signed up for. I will have to consider what this means for me that you're more invested in your stance than engaging in this conversation with me."

Let's look at a sample conversation together:

Partner A responds, "I have a mental load too. What makes yours any different from mine?"

Partner B replies, "Of course you have a mental load. I'm not denying that you do. What I keep getting confused by is what you're trying to communicate to me when you say that." PEEL THE ONION.

> **Partner A:** *"That it's not just you carrying the mental load. I do too."*
>
> **Partner B:** *"What do you need from me to know that I acknowledge and appreciate your mental load?"* PEEL THE ONION.
>
> **Partner A:** *"I don't know."*
>
> **Partner B:** *"Okay, for the record, I appreciate your mental load. I see it. My mental load doesn't discredit yours. I am still confused, though, by your response to my asking you to participate more in the load at home. What are you wanting me to take from your statement?"* PEEL THE ONION.
>
> **Partner A:** *"I'm not sure. I just feel like you're always on me about it."*
>
> **Partner B:** *"I can see that it may feel that way. When I ask and nothing changes, I feel like you don't care that I'm struggling. And then when you argue with me, it makes things feel worse. I hate feeling like a nag, but when I don't say anything I'm not sure that's any better. I just get angry inside. I wish when I spoke up you'd take me seriously and care. What are you willing to change to help us break out of this place?"* AVOID ASSUMPTION OF INTENT and COMMUNICATE RELATIONSHIP GOALS.

Being in a relationship with a resistant partner is incredibly challenging; however, I encourage you not to lose hope. I have witnessed couples, time and time again, come out of this resistance and learn to move through these conversations with much greater ease.

The Slow Grow

I want to normalize the slow grow that is almost always part of the change process in relationships. You and your partner may find yourselves making changes and feeling like you're all good—just to have something derail your progress or one of you slip back into an old pattern or habit. Our old patterns have a centripetal force; they want us to keep moving along the same path. To implement new patterns requires effort.

Have you ever been on one of those crazy spinning rides at a local fair? When I was growing up, ours was called the Scrambler, but it had a central hub with multiple spokes that split into sleigh-like seats. I'm not even sure how this thing moved—I guess it scrambled you—but I remember trying to sit forward during these rides and feeling the centripetal force pushing me back into my seat. This feeling of trying to sit up during the spin of a ride is what it can be like to implement changes in yourself and your relationship.

Keep this imagery in mind to help you and your partner have compassion for each other when you're trying to implement change. And expect setbacks along the way; they will happen, but it doesn't mean you've made zero progress.

When it comes to sharing ownership, a few things might have to give. I don't know your specific relationship situation, but here are two of the most common shifts that need to be made to involve both partners in this process:

1. The default partner may need to be more open to letting their partner share ownership.
2. The nondefault partner may need to step it up and show a real effort and interest to take on more ownership.

Making these changes will almost always involve something people tend to cringe at: asking for participation. Let's talk next about why asking is so important.

get a load of this

Personal Power

- Try to recall areas in which you may need to step back to allow your partner an opportunity to share ownership with you. Can you identify things you may do to shut down initiative taking?
- Try to identify ways in which you avoid stepping into initiative or just reinforce defaulting to your partner. Set one or two goals for increasing your initiative taking.
- If you have a resistant partner, choose one of the strategies in this chapter to try the next time you have a conversation about the mental load. It can help to write out your points beforehand so you don't get sidetracked by their defenses.

Better Together

Sometimes lack of initiative taking is just passivity that results in the default partner absorbing a task or responsibility, and other times there's something deeper going on, like worry about doing it wrong. Discuss together one specific task (do your best to depersonalize and lower defenses) and talk about what taking initiative in this area would ideally look like. Allow space for your partner to share past barriers. Troubleshoot these barriers.

CHAPTER
13

SHARE OWNERSHIP

asking is an invitation

Asking for help is a hot button issue with the mental load and one of the most common pieces of advice I hear women push back on. Their response is almost always "But I shouldn't have to ask." Up front, I want to admit that I both get it and think it's a necessary tool. Asking is important, and I'll explain why.

When I surveyed women and asked them if they ask for help when they need it, 46 percent responded that they did, even though it annoyed them. Twenty-one percent said having to ask annoyed them so they just didn't ask. I think having to ask is annoying to women for two reasons.

1. Having to Ask Implies That She Owns the Task

A woman I interviewed on the mental load recounted a story where her husband gave the kids a bath and did the dishes and then turned to her and said, "Is there anything else I can help you with today?" She got ticked off just telling me the story. She asked, he did it, and then dragged his nails across the chalkboard with the "help *you* with" statement. If she magically disappeared, these tasks would still need to be done. He'd have to hire them out or take care of them himself. Most tasks of home and family life are shared tasks; they just often are absorbed by one partner. If he views these domestic tasks as hers, then this mentality basically ensures he will never take initiative because he will just continue to stand by waiting for her commands.

Imagine telling your husband "Hey, babe, I took the kids to school, picked up dog poop, cleaned the house, thought about dinner, bought groceries, filled out permission slips for field trips, enrolled the kids in school next year, ordered Easter presents, and changed the sheets. Is there anything else I can do for *you*?"

This is no way to live. First off, it promotes a scorekeeping dynamic in the relationship. How could you *not* do these things without having a twinge of attitude and irritation? And secondly, not one person owns these tasks until you decide on that. If you signed up to have a relationship together, create a family, and live under the same roof— news flash, you're both responsible for making these worlds go round.

2. He Should Know

This is the point most often emphasized by women I have talked with about the mental load. If you recall my own stories throughout this book, you could argue that some of the things Chad may have missed were things he should already know because they seem like they're common sense.

- He should know how to figure out ordering balloons.
- He should know to bring towels to the pool.

This point feels delicate to make because, yes, many of these things are common sense and so it's hard to justify the lack of initiative. On the other hand, when the roles of default versus nondefault have been unintentionally locked in, the nondefault partner tends to turn off common sense and rely on their partner for orders and lists. The overwhelming worry of "doing it wrong" shuts down their initiative and increases their dependence on their partner for telling them what to do. And the lack of emotional labor invested by the nondefault partner tends to stunt their initiative or lower their standards so dramatically that they've been corrected or "criticized," so they opt out of thinking for themselves and continue to defer to the default partner.

HER PERSPECTIVE

I struggle to ask for help or delegate and eventually melt down or explode, which finally forces us to talk about my overwhelm. My husband has said it hurts him to see this reoccurring pain, and he tried to help but doesn't see/think of so many things that I do, so it's difficult to not repeat the cycle.

This dynamic is detrimental to the relationship and typically requires each partner to step toward the other. The default partner has to be willing to express their desires clearly and ask for what they want. The nondefault partner needs to increase their investment in learning what needs done and how it needs done and in not being afraid to suggest a solution and potentially have it be edited by their partner. It's not personal—consider it a learning opportunity.

It makes sense if the concept of asking bugs you. I get that. But I hope you are a little more open to asking for help in order to shift the mental load. Of course, it requires more than just asking; both partners have to participate. This is important for four reasons:

1. **Piling on precedents.** You take it on; he checks out. Once that happens, unloading a task requires taking it from invisible to visible for him. (Remember this from chapter 4?) The pattern has to be reversed, and part of making things visible is asking.
2. **Your partner isn't a mind reader.** Cliché? Yes. But this reminder needs to be said. Your partner doesn't always know your expectations or standards. They don't know the internal plan you have for what you want done. Let them in your head so they can be involved.

3. **Set your partner up for success.** Asking gives your partner an opportunity to get it right. It's also a kindness to yourself to invite support. When you don't ask, you ensure the outcome is no support. When you do ask, you're giving your partner the option to step up.

4. **Your standards may be different.** You have your way of doing things and standards for how you like them done. Don't assume your partner carries the same standards or even knows what yours are.

I want to call out one major mistake I see partners making when it comes to being annoyed at asking: They make an assumption of intention. It's easy to assume that a partner's lack of initiative means he is resistant to taking on more of the mental load. But when you make this assumption, it impacts the story you tell yourself about your partner. You start to see him as a jerk who doesn't want to help out. What is likely more accurate is that your partner is passively willing. They aren't resistant but they aren't taking initiative so they just sit back and wait for your commands. I'm not suggesting this isn't frustrating, but the way you and your partner work together changes if they are passively willing versus actively resistant. Here's a visual of what I'm talking about. This is the same continuum of participation from chapter 12.

Continuum of participation

Resistant to helping	Passive willingness	Takes initiative

I've often said that "asking" needs to be rebranded to "involving." Asking is an invitation for your partner to step into your world; it reveals expectations, and it can help a partner learn how something is done (that they typically haven't done before) so that they can move along the continuum toward initiative taking, which is the ultimate goal. Asking is a stepping stone toward the goal of initiative taking because it takes the invisible aspects of the mental load and brings them into a shared awareness. This allows a couple to then revisit who does what, what needs to be done, and how it gets done instead of continuing to perpetuate the same pattern of one person carrying it without the other sharing it.

When you think about how to incorporate asking into your dynamic with your partner, know there are two primary ways you can do this.

1. **In the moment:** "Hey, can you pack up the diaper bag before we head out?" Tone matters on this one.

2. **In advance:** "Tomorrow I want you to be in charge of packing the diaper bag before we head out. Do you have any questions?" Prompting for questions helps deal with any potential issues that come up the next day and also helps you avoid the "I'll just do it myself" syndrome. Another take on this one is "Tomorrow I want you to be in charge of the diaper bag before we head out. Will you run through what needs to be in there out loud in case I have anything to add?" Take into consideration what you know about your partner on this suggestion. Some people may take this as condescending, but others may appreciate being able to check their work ahead of time and also knowing exactly how it should be done.

A common question for nondefault partners is "How can I help?" Please know that some people have more sensitivity than others to the idea of "helping." Remember, helping suggests that whatever it is belongs to her until she delegates it. There are plenty of ways to ask how you can help that don't trigger this irritation and also prompt deeper knowing so that next time you can take care of it without having to ask.

"HOW CAN I HELP?" REPLACEMENT PHRASES

Instead of	Try
"What do you want me to do?"	"Can you show me how you like this done? That way I don't have to ask next time."

"Just tell me what to do."	"I want to be able to help you, but I'm not sure what's on your mental list for the day. I wish I could read your mind. Can you share with me how I can help today?"
"Just tell me what to do."	"What's on your plate for today? Oh! Let me take *this* or *that* off it for you."
"Just ask when you need help."	"I don't like to see you struggle on your own; I just don't know what to do. You're not alone in this."
"What should I do about XYZ?"	Offering solutions then asking for revisions. For example, "I was thinking about the party we have this week and thought I'd take care of cleaning the decks. Does this sound good, or do you have something else you want me to prioritize?"

There will be times where the default partner will still decide not to ask and will just take care of it on their own. However, I want you to work to increase your asking with the long-term goal of prompting greater initiative. When you feel annoyed by having to ask, here are some reframes to consider.

REMINDERS WHEN YOU'RE ANNOYED ABOUT ASKING

Instead of	Try
"It's easier to do it myself than to explain."	"If I talk it out, it allows my partner to enter into my world versus keeping it all to myself. How can they help if they don't know what I want done?"
"I shouldn't have to ask."	"Asking is a part of undoing the responsibilities that typically default to me. When I explain or ask, I make the invisible visible."
"Asking means I'm failing. I should be able to do it all."	"No one can do it all on their own and not suffer some sort of consequences. Asking is a kindness to myself and pushes back against a deeply engrained belief that I should be able to do it all."

Now that we've unpacked the importance of asking your partner to share ownership, let's unpack how certain behaviors—from the default or nondefault partner—can really backfire and what you can do to avoid those behaviors as you move forward.

get a load of this

Personal Power

- Come up with an in-the-moment reframe or mantra when you're tempted to not ask your partner to step up and instead do it yourself.
- Check your attitude when you're asked to do something. Do you respond with a happy willingness or an eye roll? Your nonverbals matter and will either prompt more asking or build resentment in your partner.
- Check your attitude when you ask. Do you do it with irritation and condescension? Make sure you're not dishing out attitude you don't want to get in return.

Better Together

What are some of the barriers that come up around asking? Discuss them together with curiosity and talk about how you can approach asking differently in the future.

CHAPTER
14

avoiding behaviors that backfire

When it comes to taking ownership over the mental load, there are some behaviors that get in the way of either stepping in and taking more initiative or getting out of the way so your partner can develop competency and confidence by taking more on. For the default partner, I am going to lay out five behaviors that backfire. And for the nondefault partner, I'm going to describe a concept called *weaponized incompetence*. If you're reading this alone, I hope this offers some perspective as you reflect on your role. If you're reading this together, I hope you can both approach this section with some humility and humor because I'm going to call both partners out.

Behaviors That Backfire When You're the Default Partner

There are five common behaviors that can undermine your efforts to hand over parts of the mental load. When you engage in any of these behaviors, they lead to a feeling of walking on eggshells for your partner. These behaviors often lead to your partner telling themselves the story of "I never get it right so why even try." I'd bet one or all of them will be familiar to you.

1. **Impatience:** You ask your partner to do something and then if it isn't done in the allotted time (that usually exists in your head), you will take care of it yourself, perpetuating the notion that you've got a handle on things and will just do it if he doesn't. Stop bailing your partner out.

2. **Keeping Score:** Your partner does something but you remind them that you still do more. "Thanks, babe, but that's a drop in the bucket compared to what I do." This is a surefire way to sour the tone in your relationship and for your partner to say, "Why bother" or "It's never enough." Try to incorporate a spirit of regularly acknowledging contributions and progress. It feels good to be seen and appreciated, so do this for each other more—you won't give your partner the upper hand or a big head by just saying thank you.

3. **Micromanaging:** You ask your partner to do something and then are on their case while they try to do it, critiquing them along the way. If you want to control the process, then do it yourself or ask if you can teach them how to do it. But hanging over their shoulder doing a play-by-play analysis is not going to facilitate their taking more on. If you need to, just leave the room.

4. **Criticizing:** Your partner does something but then you pick it apart. It may sound like "Thanks for getting the kids dressed, but geez, what are they wearing?" If you placed yourself on the receiving end of feedback like this, how would it feel? I bet that it would shut down future participation and perpetuate the feeling of walking on eggshells anytime you try to handle a task.

5. **Personalization:** You interpret your partner's actions as a personal attack. "I see you didn't do the dishes again; I guess you don't care about how tired I am." It's important not to make assumptions about these things without checking them, or work to offer a gracious interpretation and disconnect the idea that everything is about you.

In order to revise your behaviors that backfire, you have to identify which ones get stirred up for you. When you feel triggered, it's important to have a plan for how to manage this moment. When you're "in the moment," it's way too hard to make a plan because you're likely feeling irritated, mad, or unsurprised because it's the same old crap again. Next time, be prepared to handle it differently in order to create space for changes to occur. See the example and exercise below for how to do this.

My behavior that backfires	My plan for when I'm triggered
Micromanaging	The next time I am triggered to tell my partner how to do something or to correct him in the moment, I will remind myself that he is doing his best. That this is new and that I want him to take more on. Then I will determine if what I need to tell him is important or if I can just let it go.

I want to highlight what you can do instead of engaging in the behaviors that backfire, and that is to give your partner an F. The three F's of handing over part of the mental load are allowing your partner to

- fail,
- figure it out, and
- fine-tune.

Think of it like this: If you hand over packing lunch for your daughter who is just starting fifth grade but you've done it up until this point, just run the numbers. On average kids go to school 180 days a year times five years (kindergarten through the beginning of fifth grade), which totals around nine hundred lunches. You've had a lot of practice to figure out the most efficient and best way of packing lunches for your daughter. Let your partner have the space to figure it out too. They may fail, and that's okay. They will need time to fine-tune. And that's okay too—give them the space and time to do that. This is a hard thing to reflect on, but it's necessary. How many times have you enabled your partner by taking care of things instead of letting them do it or by rescuing them from learning how to do it on their own? Give them an F and get out of their way!

Behaviors That Backfire When You're the Nondefault Partner

Weaponized incompetence is a term that describes, typically, a man's tendency to feign incompetence or use incompetence as an excuse so they don't have to take care of things that are typically associated with the mental load. To be honest, I don't love this term because it implies that the intention is to weaponize this. And I think that assuming negative intentions is a quick way to get into a bad attitude about your partner, which causes all sorts of other issues. But the reality is that many men intentionally or unintentionally do this. So, if you're the nondefault partner reading this, I hope you can approach it with a non-defensive stance, and if you're the default partner, I'll offer some suggestions about what you can do about this.

Let me describe what this looks like:

1. **Weaponized incompetence:** Someone uses their "lack of skill or knowing" as an excuse not to do something. It usually sounds like "You're just better at it than I am."
2. **Weaponized delaying:** The partner delays doing a task and

then their partner takes care of it for them. It usually sounds like "I said I'd do it."

3. **Weaponized amnesia:** The partner says they don't remember being asked to do something, where something goes or is, or aspects of the family's life or schedule. It usually sounds like "I don't remember you telling me to do that."

4. **Weaponized complication:** A task is perceived as too complicated for the partner to do it, or they make it more complicated, so it "makes sense" that you just take it on. It could sound like "I'd take them to the dentist, but I may have to move some things around and they like it best when you're there. Oh, and where is it again?"

If you read any of these and feel a little called out, it's okay. I'm glad they're on your radar and now you can step into the revision phase and start to take more initiative.

In order to combat weaponized incompetence as the nondefault partner, you have to be aware of what happens in your home and of the members of your family. My dad and I used to have a podcast (the *Love Thinks* podcast) and we once interviewed a couple on the mental load. The husband shared an incredibly important piece of information that he incorporated into his role as a father and husband. He said, "I think of myself as a data collector. As I drive the girls home from school and I listen to their conversations, I think, *What can I learn about them to help take things on, care for them better, support them, and share with my wife?*" Increased information helps to inform initiative taking. You cannot take initiative unless you know how your home and family functions.

If you aren't the default partner, then it likely means you're less "in the know" in your family life. What this means is that you simply need to increase your knowing. You do this by paying more attention and being intentional about recording the details that you observe and hear. If you aren't good at remembering, make a note in your phone. Another way to know more is to ask more questions. I know this sounds like common sense, but if you don't ask questions about your home and family life, you will not know what's going on. It's not rocket science; it's just increasing your awareness because your family and home life are important and you can love your family better when you know them deeply. Knowing facilitates initiative taking.

If this feels too vague, adopt the Buffett Formula: Go to bed smarter than you woke up. Warren Buffett applied this formula to the accumulation of knowledge. He said, "All of us can build our knowledge, but most of us won't put in the effort."[1] When you work to build a little more knowledge today than you had yesterday about your partner, home, and family life it builds like compound interest, making you a little more in the know today than yesterday.

HER PERSPECTIVE

I am resentful that he has it much easier but still complains. I don't want to tell him to do the things; I want him to think of what needs to be done every day and just do some of it.

I've shared with you that my husband, Chad, travels almost every week. But we once had a stretch after the holidays where he didn't travel for almost eight weeks. It was eye-opening how different our family functioned when he was present to be a data collector. He knew the schedules, he knew what the kids wanted for breakfast, he was in the know. If you're a partner who travels, works shifts, deploys, or has an unusual schedule, you will have to work harder at this. Here are several ways to do this.

STAY CONNECTED WHEN YOU'RE APART

- Share a digital schedule using an app, your phones, or products like Skylight digital calendars so you all know what's going on when (FYI: For partners with ADHD a digital calendar can be a game changer).

- Have a family journal or shared journal with the parent/partner who travels. This way you can write to one another when you're apart and exchange it when they return home. I ask our kids, "Was there a time today when you needed me but I wasn't with you?" This is a prompt that can come in handy.
- Have a designated debriefing time as a family and/or as a couple when the partner reintegrates into family life. This can help the partner get caught up on what they missed and be more in the know.

How to Deal with Weaponized Incompetence as the Default Partner

If you are the default partner reading this, here are some tips for dealing with weaponized incompetence and some scripts that may come in handy.

- **Starve it vs. feed it:** Starving this type of behavior means that you don't bail them out every time they hesitate or give some attitude. Yes, it may require some thicker skin or calling the response out, but every time you feed the behavior it grows.
- **Give them time to learn their own way:** You've likely had a lot of practice with a particular task. If they're new or "incompetent," give them the time and space to figure it out on their own. If they try to pass the buck, offer some encouragement, but *do not* take it on.
- **Train them on specific tasks . . . within reason:** I would bet there are some things you prefer to be done a particular way. If there are tasks that you're handing over but you have specific standards, walk your partner through the task (not every time, but once). If they still claim to not know how, then the discussion becomes, "I walked you through how to do this already. What were you missing and what can help you remember moving forward?"

SCRIPTS FOR ADDRESSING WEAPONIZED INCOMPETENCE

Type: Weaponized incompetence	
Statement: "You're so much better at it than I am."	
Script for reply	"I know you think I'm better at it than you, but I've just had more practice. I didn't know how to do all of this naturally; I had to learn through trial and error. I'm happy to show you once what I do if you'd like, but I'm not okay with you saying you can't because you aren't as good at it as me. That just leaves me alone to take care of it all the time and I don't want to be the sole person to carry this burden."
Type: Weaponized delaying	
Statement: "I'll get to it in a minute" (but never does).	
Script for reply	"I've noticed that when I ask for your help with something you tend to delay and then I end up taking care of it. This leaves me with frustration toward you because I put the effort into asking and then I still have to put the effort into doing. We need a better way to handle these situations. What ideas do you have? Also, I'm making a commitment to *not* do the thing I'm asking you to do, even if it means it doesn't get done."
Type: Weaponized complication	
Statement: "Hmm, my schedule is really tight . . ."; "I don't know where it is . . ."; "You're more used to doing this than I am . . ."	
Script for reply	"Wow, that sounds really complicated. When you say all the barriers out loud it's hard to not feel a pull to just take it on myself. But I'm not going to do that this time. I get that it's hard and not always convenient, but I'm really grateful for what you're doing."
Type: Weaponized amnesia	
Statement: "I don't remember you telling me to do that."	
Script for reply	"I've noticed that we are remembering things differently. I know I asked you to do ___ but I can't prove that I'm right or you are. Let's just agree moving forward that you write it down or set a reminder in your phone so we don't keep having this discussion."

Responding clearly in the moment and calling out the backfiring behavior—whether it's intentional or not—will help you continue that slow grow of getting to a better ownership share.

I've covered a few behaviors that backfire, but now it's time to focus on three behaviors to adopt as you move forward.

Ask, Act, Appreciate

When you're doing the work to shift the mental load in your relationship, it is really important to be clear about what you actually want to change. This may sound obvious but sharing ownership around the mental load can feel a bit arbitrary. What are we sharing? What does it mean to take initiative? What does "right" look like? Whenever there are complications, it slows progress. To help you home in on what you may want to shift so you can express it clearly, I am going to outline three behaviors of ownership that are most important.

1. Asking
2. Action
3. Appreciation (see chapter 7 for the formula)

When you're preparing to talk to your partner or are reading through this, consider what you want from your partner in these three areas. Note that it may be adding something, subtracting something, or multiplying something you're already doing. If you're the nondefault partner, maybe you want your default partner to speak up more and make their desires known. If you're the default partner, maybe you want your partner to ask you more often what's on your plate so they can take initiative. Maybe you need to see more action-oriented initiative or maybe you just need to feel appreciated and seen. These things go both ways and you may crave any of these or all of them. Also, when you're the default partner, consider what this looks like when it's done just how you imagine it. As I've mentioned before, if you caught on camera what "right" looked like, what would the viewer see? Get as specific as possible.

Request	Example	Caught on camera
ASKING	NONDEFAULT: "I wish you'd just ask me for help more."	When you feel stressed, you pause and look at me and say, "I need you."
ASKING	DEFAULT: "I wish you'd check in on me more."	Before I even get stressed, you notice I need you to step in, and say, "What's something I can take off your plate today?"
ACTION	NONDEFAULT: "I wish you'd write down exactly what you need me to do."	When you need me to take on a task or responsibility, you have a list or note ready.
ACTION	DEFAULT: "I wish that you'd prep all the water bottles before we leave the house."	Within ten minutes of having to leave, you gather the kids' water bottles and refill them and make sure they are by the door.
APPRECIATION	NONDEFAULT: "I wish that you'd seem more excited to see me."	When I get home at the end of the day, you stop what you're doing and give me a big kiss and say that you missed me.
APPRECIATION	DEFAULT: "I wish that you'd express gratitude for all I do more often."	You pull me into a hug and kiss my cheek and say, "You're so incredible. With all that you carry, I'm so grateful for you."

get a load of this

Personal Power

- Pay attention to how you collect data around the home and family life. How can you make sure you're doing more of this? Are there systems or strategies you can put in place to make sure you stay on top of this?
- Can you identify any of the weaponized incompetence behaviors in your own actions? Set a goal for how to do this less often or eliminate it for good.
- Can you identify any behaviors that backfire that you regularly participate in? Make a plan for engaging in these less often.

Better Together

- Come up with an agreed-upon plan or code word for when you suspect your partner is engaging in weaponized incompetence or a behavior that backfires. How can you kindly call each other out and work together to stop this pattern?
- Work to increase expression of appreciation. End this conversation with sharing something you appreciate about each other. You can't do this too often.

CHAPTER
15

SHARE ACCOUNTABILITY

for yourself

Sharing accountability means you have agreements for how
you conduct yourselves and handle the mental load that you
can return to when things get messed up.

For the first ten years of marriage, I procrastinated when it came
to having difficult conversations with Chad. I have this ability to
swivel perspectives, which is a gift I'm happy to possess but can also
leave me confused and dizzy after entertaining too many people's
points of view.

Fortunately, I've learned how to be more grounded in the things
that matter to me, but for a very long time I would wait to bring things
up until after I had sat with them for way too long. Basically, I brought
things up past their expiration date and usually right before bed or
sex. If you're thinking, *Me too!*, that makes sense. It is actually pretty
common for us to do this because sleep and sex are two points of our
day we feel safer entering into after connection. Also, if you have kids,
it can feel like the only time you're alone to talk.

Chad would almost always sigh, visibly annoyed, and remind me how I have a knack for bringing things up at the worst times. I would attempt to justify it by reminding him that we barely see each other or we've been so busy or it's just never a good time.

Here's the important thing: I am responsible for how I show up in my relationship. I am responsible for sharing my feelings and needs and not waiting until they build up. We sometimes forget this in our relationships, because pointing the finger is so much easier: "I wouldn't do this *if* you didn't do that." There is something rather instinctual about the tendency to defend oneself, but it just isn't conducive to our relationships.

Self-Accountability

In a perfect world we would all come to our relationships as fully actualized human beings. Armed with insight, ready to love without hesitation, prepared to steep ourselves in vulnerability, and determined to love our partners with our guards down. Unfortunately, we are imperfect human beings bringing our baggage into relationships, armed with defenses, ready to love with a tinge of hesitation, and determined to care for our partners as long as they're caring for us in the ways we want. When we show up in our relationships, we carry with us the programming from experiences. In the chapters on expectations, I explained how we all have parts of ourselves that don't fully blossom until the right conditions occur, and these conditions may not always bring out the best in you or your partner. But in order to be accountable for how you show up in your relationship, you have to develop some insight into what your relationship-wrecker behaviors may be.

An accusation that Chad would frequently insert into our "arguments" was that I was taking things personally. We'd be talking about whatever, and if I started to get a little fired up, he'd say, "You're taking this so personally." In my defense, sometimes things are personal in heated discussions. Especially when I'd hear the story Chad was telling himself about me, yet I didn't feel it was fair or accurate. At the same time, his statement wasn't untrue, but rather it was grounded in his experiences with me.

I am a highly sensitive person (HSP)—not that I'm easily offended, but that I pick up on sensory changes very easily. If I walk into a room and there's anything off, I soak it up like a sponge. You may resonate with this, and if you do, I highly recommend reading *The Highly Sensitive Person* by Elaine Aron. I tend to be more sensitive to sounds, smells, and any slight change in my environment. It's equal parts awesome and annoying. The superpower of HSPs is that we are very attuned to other people's emotions and needs and, because of this, tension in someone else feels like it's tension directed at us. For years, to appease my discomfort when I would read someone else as "off," I'd ask if everything was okay, followed by "Did I do something?" and then I'd top it off with "Are you upset with me?" In reality, it's actually quite annoying. I was constantly temperature-checking to see if things were safe and okay, and most of the time the other person's change in mood had nothing to do with me.

My constant personalization was exhausting for me and for my husband and any other person who it was directed toward. I had to take accountability for how I was showing up in my relationships for my good and for everyone else's. This was on me, so I committed to personalizing less, which in turn allowed me to show up much lighter to my relationships and created more ease between Chad and me. If I hadn't been willing to take a look at how I was showing up, I would have missed this opportunity to make a positive change in our relationship.

You are accountable for how *you* show up in your relationship, and taking inventory of your behaviors requires that you have some level of humility and willingness to change. You are responsible for managing yourself and have the power to make changes in this area, without your partner doing a thing.

Remember, you can expend your energy trying to convince your partner that you're right, that you don't need to change a thing, and that their perspective isn't valid, or you can expend your energy trying to make your relationship better. It's your choice. Each person has some level of power to shift the dynamic in their relationship. This chapter will lay out two areas of accountability you should consider as an individual: how you engage in relationship-wrecking responses and how you express your needs.

You must know that the nine behaviors that follow are sure to downshift your relationship. One of the first steps to addressing self-accountability is to increase your awareness of what you're doing that may be causing issues. I often say that the less insight you have, the more defenses you'll use. I'm going to outline nine relationship-wrecking behaviors to raise your insight so you can be empowered to choose a different approach.

Nine Relationship-Wrecking Responses

These behaviors may show up during difficult conversations or just during your daily interactions with your partner. By this point in the book, my hope is that you've gained some insights as to why you may engage in some of these behaviors, but now it's time to really label them and make a change. As you read through these, reflect on how you show up in your relationship and consider how you can take some accountability to make changes. Some of these have already been explored in previous chapters, but I want to remind you of them again.

1. Dismiss

This response can occur during major disagreements or during regular interactions throughout the day. When you dismiss your partner, to them it can feel like you don't care, you aren't invested in what they're saying, or you devalue them. Ultimately when you dismiss a partner, you leave them alone in their experience. Here are some examples of dismissive statements and behaviors.

> **Partner 1:** *"Gosh, I'm so tired from the day. I feel like I was 'on' all day."*

> **Partner 2:** *"Well, I'm pretty tired from my day too."*

This is dismissive because Partner 1 is looking for something, maybe just acknowledgment or empathy or even appreciation. Partner 2 responds with a statement about their own fatigue, without offering any acknowledgment to their partner.

> **Partner 1:** *"I miss you. I feel like we never really connect anymore."*
>
> **Partner 2:** *"Yeah, we're just so busy."*

This is dismissive because Partner 1 is looking to connect and to know that their partner is missing them too, yet Partner 2 doesn't offer any affectionate words in return. Not only is it a missed opportunity, but it can actually cause some hurt.

2. Defend

This reaction usually occurs during more difficult conversations, but it can spring up during normal conversation, surprising an unsuspecting partner. Defensiveness is basically a reaction to feeling like you're being unjustly accused or characterized or it's a response when you're protecting yourself from the pain and responsibility associated with admitting that you've wronged someone. The painful and infuriating thing about defending is that it shifts the blame onto your partner. In order to excuse yourself from taking the blame, it has to go somewhere else. Another effect is that defensiveness can shift the focus of the conversation. If one partner shares a hurt and the other responds with defensiveness, the hurt partner now may be pushed to console the partner who got defensive. It becomes focused on one partner instead of relationship-centric. Overall, this erodes a sense of trust and security in the relationship. Consider what may be eliciting a defensive response from you. Here are some examples.

> **Partner 1:** *"I thought you were going to pick Caleb up from soccer."*
>
> **Partner 2:** *"You didn't communicate that clearly; you should have reminded me."*

Partner 2 took this question immediately as a criticism and then shifted the blame onto Partner 1. A seemingly simple comment from Partner 1 likely will evolve into a full-blown argument, leaving both partners hurt, feeling misunderstood, and wary about the relationship. This could have easily been avoided if Partner 2 would have simply accepted responsibility.

Partner 1: *"I felt really hurt by what you said."*

Partner 2: *"I guess I just never get it right with you."*

Partner 1 is opening up to Partner 2 by expressing a hurt, and this takes a level of vulnerability. Partner 2's response shifts the focus from their part in the hurt to their own sense of being victimized. This conversation can go a number of ways, but potentially Partner 1 may expend way too much energy (when already hurting) to reassure Partner 2. Or Partner 1 may fly off the handle in utter frustration, blowing this entire conversation up. If Partner 2 would just listen, explore what it was that hurt Partner 1, or take some responsibility, likely this conversation would go smoothly and lead to increased connection instead of more division.

3. Distancing

This behavior can occur during a difficult conversation or even in the relationship when you're hurting. In a difficult conversation, distancing can look like shutting down and disengaging from talking about it anymore. It can also occur when someone gets their feelings hurt or is offended, and then they just throw their hands up and detach. Distancing outside the moment is a silent relationship killer. This is when someone has unresolved hurts or unmet needs and decides to keep them inside but pulls away and detaches their feelings from their partner.

All of these distancing responses are damaging to a relationship and painful to experience for both partners. Something worth mentioning is that the partner who is doing the distancing is almost always doing it to find some sense of security. That partner is basically saying, "I'll leave before you can hurt me," but it ends up creating more hurts and disconnection rather than offering the protection and safety they're seeking. Please note that asking for a break from a difficult conversation is *not* the same as distancing. I'll cover that in the next point.

> **Partner 1:** *"I really need to talk about this with you. It's important to me."*
>
> **Partner 2:** *"I'm done. This is pointless."*

In this scenario, Partner 1 would probably feel unimportant, invisible, and that their needs most likely aren't being met in the way they want. A common response would be for them to start to detach. Partner 2 checked out after the initial conversation and will probably be unclear as to why their partner is disconnecting. They may feel the shift, but they won't know why. Overall, Partner 2 is communicating a message that says, "Your needs don't matter to me."

> **Partner 1:** *"It hurt my feelings when you said that to me the other day."*
>
> **Partner 2:** *"I guess I'm the worst. I just won't talk to you anymore then."* Then proceeds to give the silent treatment.

Partner 2 is protecting themselves from feeling the guilt or responsibility for hurting their partner's feelings. They may also think that their partner is being too sensitive. When Partner 2 checks out and then ices out Partner 1, they are inadvertently communicating that their partner's feelings don't matter to them. Partner 2 is also shifting the attention to themselves rather than showing concern for their partner. This will erode a sense of reliability and security in the relationship.

4. Pursue relentlessly

This is the opposite of the distancer. This person pursues relentlessly to the point that it doesn't give their partner an opportunity to process information or get space when they need it. During difficult conversations, it can be helpful for one or both partners to hit pause and take a break in order to regulate themselves or gather their thoughts. Sometimes discussions aren't going anywhere and a break is necessary, but the pursuer doesn't allow their partner to take this space. They can't handle the anxiety of disconnection or someone being upset with them and so they aggressively and relentlessly pursue working it out. Ultimately, this behavior tends to push their partner away, causing *more* distance—the thing they're most worried about. A pursuer is also looking for security and safety, but they are going about it in a way that will likely make their fear of distance a reality.

> **Partner 1:** *"Hey, I need to take a break and come back to this."*

> **Partner 2:** *"When? How long? We need to work this out now!"*

Partner 1 is being very clear about what they need, but Partner 2 isn't honoring that. Likely their anxiety is through the roof and they can't allow the break due to their own discomfort. Partner 2 will have to learn how to regulate and manage their own anxiety in order to allow Partner 1 time and space to settle down and process. Both partners would benefit from an agreed-upon time to come back together to finish the discussion. Sometimes partners feel anxious about the break because the conversation never gets completed, so Partner 1 should offer reassurance to Partner 2 that they will return to finish things and can even provide a specific amount of time this break will last.

5. Personalize

This response is closely related to defensiveness, but instead of everything being the other person's fault, the partner assumes everything is about them. The way that they interpret and make meaning of their partner's behavior, words, or inaction is personalized. This means that they're going to easily create a storyline where they are the victim and their partner is the perpetrator, and they will quickly develop a bad attitude toward their partner. Also, someone who personalizes everything becomes very difficult to talk to during a tough conversation because the talk will regularly get derailed by trying to convince them it had nothing to do with them. It can be exhausting.

> **Partner 1:** *Sees dirty dishes in the sink and thinks, It's like they don't even care about me and expect me to do everything around here. If they did care about me, these would already be done.*

I guarantee you that Partner 1's attitude toward their partner instantly turned negative. Remember from chapter 11 on sharing expectations, you're in charge of revising your story about your partner. Avoid walking around the house collecting complaints—you will find plenty of opportunities to be ticked off at your partner, if that's how you want to feel toward them. Do your best to care for your attitude and pay special attention to how you personalize things in your relationship.

6. Power Moves

A power move is when a partner attempts to position themselves in a more supreme place, making the other partner feel small. In abusive relationships, most of the dynamics revolve around power. I'm not suggesting that any power move is an abusive relationship, but if you're in an abusive relationship, power moves will definitely be present. Sometimes power moves show up as criticism, judgment, or passive-aggressiveness (which is almost always a power move). This behavior makes one partner feel powerful while the other is put in their place or made to feel insignificant, invalidated, and invisible.

> **Partner 1:** *"I'm so tired. Can you give me a little time this weekend?"*

> **Partner 2:** *"How are you tired? You just take care of the kids. I work all week and am responsible for hundreds of employees."*

In this exchange, Partner 1 is expressing a need and a request and Partner 2's response insinuates that Partner 1 doesn't have a right to be tired or take time on their own. Partner 2's response minimizes Partner 1's feelings, exhaustion, and right to breaks by comparing them to their own output, suggesting what they do is far more exhausting and important. This is a surefire way to damage a relationship. In the end, hard is hard, tired is tired—it doesn't really matter who has it worse. What matters is that you both come to each other and get the support, acknowledgment, and empathy you both deserve.

> **Partner 1:** *Has a big event and Partner 2 agreed to watch the kids.*
>
> **Partner 2:** *"Oh, I forgot. I made plans tonight to go to a work dinner."*

Partner 2's behavior reads as passive-aggressive. This type of behavior is very difficult to navigate because you have to rely on the person doing it to actually admit what they're doing. Partner 1 has an important choice here. They can cancel their plans, push back on Partner 2, or call Partner 2 out. All of these choices will almost certainly create tension in the relationship.

7. Point Fingers

When a partner points fingers, they accuse their partner of acting in a way that pigeonholes them, making it difficult to have a productive conversation. This is essentially name calling, labeling a partner, or overgeneralizing. Pointing fingers can also mean simply blaming the other person. This one shows up all the time with kids.

> **Partner 1:** *"I'm so overwhelmed with all I have to do for work this week."*
>
> **Partner 2:** *"Geez, you're so dramatic about it. You just make a bigger deal out of things than necessary."*

These responses always baffle me and make me wonder what someone is trying to achieve with them. I can assure you that Partner 1 feels dismissed, misunderstood, undervalued, and will become less and less likely to confide in their partner. It's these minor interactions that add up over time and lead to major disconnections.

8. Passivity

Passivity can show up when a partner just shoves everything down. They may think their partner won't meet their needs, or they've asked and their partner doesn't show up to meet their needs, or they placate their partner to get by in the relationship, or they've given up and are just going through the motions. These behaviors guarantee a particular outcome, which is disconnection and likely a very unhappy relationship. If you have not expressed your needs, it's time to learn how. If you hold it all in, you're setting yourself up for a potential future blowup or you may later walk away from the relationship when the kids have grown. Learning how to assert yourself in your relationship is necessary if you're someone who tends to lean toward passivity.

> **Partner 1:** *"I thought dinner would have been ready by now."*
>
> **Partner 2:** *Feels hurt and unseen because their day was hard and there are reasons that they are behind in making dinner. But Partner 2 doesn't express any of this and just responds with "I'm sorry; I'm hurrying." Also consider that Partner 1 may not have meant anything negative by this statement and Partner 2 may have missed an opportunity to understand their partner better as well as be understood better.*

9. Painful Statements

This last relationship-wrecking behavior is all too common. It involves one partner saying something in the heat of the moment, even though they may not really mean it. Again, this seems like common sense.

Don't we regularly tell our kids, "You can be mad, but you can't speak to me that way"? It's wild how the basic understanding of proper human behavior and treatment go out the window in our most intimate relationships. Here's the rub with this one: The partner on the receiving end can't unhear what was said in the heat of the moment. Maybe their partner didn't really mean it, but the words exist and are imprinted on their mind and heart.

> **Partner 1:** *"I'm really hurting after what you said to me earlier today."*
>
> **Partner 2:** *"That's not my responsibility. You're so sensitive— just get over it. Sometimes you're just too much for me."*

Partner 1 attempted to share something in order to repair a hurt and foster connection. Now Partner 1 will have a layered hurt based on Partner 2's response. They will also now be aware that their partner thinks these things about them, which will have a lasting impact on their feeling of security and safety in the relationship.

Words are a reflection of someone's thoughts and their heart. Make sure you choose your words carefully and bite your tongue when you feel the urge to spew nastiness toward your partner that you ultimately don't really mean. They may just believe it.

Part of shifting these tendencies is the ability to recognize them. Think about how you respond during these important moments. The next step is to change your behavior by inserting another response. Instead of defending, what can you do instead? How can you start to reshape how you show up in your relationship? The last step is to reinforce this new behavior with repeating the new responses over and over. Will you slip up? Sure you will. But that's just part of the process. And please note, many of these behaviors occur during moments of high emotion.

This will require that you work to regulate yourself enough to make a solid choice. Sometimes all it takes is deep and slow breaths, but there's no shortage of emotional regulation tactics available online. Work through the How You Show Up Exercise (also found with the QR code in the Additional Resources) to help identify and change how you show up in your relationship.

How You Show Up Exercise

If you recognize how you show up, list out some of your relationship-wrecking responses here:

_____

_____

_____

If you don't recognize how you show up, reflect on the following questions:

- What does my partner accuse me of most? Can I identify some truth in the accusations? Where?
- When my partner approaches me with a need, my immediate response is to _____.

Ways I can change how I show up:

- Ask for a pause.
- Fact-check your assumptions.
- Restate what your partner said.
- Take notes and regulate before responding.
- Take four deep breaths (google "box breathing" for tips).
- Explain how you're feeling in the moment before responding to content.

My plan for the next time I'm tempted to respond in a relationship-wrecking way is to

_____

_____

Express Your Needs

Throughout the book I've explained how both men and women tend to struggle with expressing needs due to different but impactful socializations. Remember, men are socialized to be self-reliant, strong, and unemotional. Women are socialized to put others' needs before their own, and they are great at intuiting needs, which means they end up meeting the needs of others despite the "others" not expressing them. Both partners have to take accountability for learning how to identify and assert their needs in a loving and respectful way.

This skill is so important because when you don't speak your needs, you make the decision for your partner. You make the decision not to let them show up for you or care for you in the way you need. You make the decision to martyr yourself, and the result is often resentment. It's not fair to you or the people you love to withhold your needs and then resent them for not meeting those needs. I realize this is a bit of tough love, but it must be said; you and your relationships are too important.

For years in my relationship, I would tell Chad I wanted more romance. Looking back it's sort of funny how vague that really is. Many times our needs are expressed in broad and unspecific terms that set our partner up for failure.

Yes, there are partners who don't change. Yes, there are partners who are resistant to meeting needs, but keep in mind that oftentimes the way the need is expressed is unclear. For years, Chad would nod his head and say, "Okay, got it," and then nothing would happen. Or I'd get flowers that week and then it was back to status quo. What I had to learn was that if I'm not clear, I'm just confusing. My vague request for romance didn't make sense. What's romantic to me may not be romantic to the next person. There's personal style, preference, and parameters built into this request that I never expressed. The same goes for your relationship. If you or your partner aren't clear, how are you both supposed to know how to meet the other's needs?

Here are a few rules of thumb for asserting your needs:

- Try to balance assertiveness with grace and compliments. Assertiveness doesn't have to mean gruff or angry.
- Be clear and specific (but you should know this by now).
- Try not to blame or be critical.
- Use the "more of something" approach versus the "you don't do this at all" approach.

Here are some scripts to get you started.

TO YOUR PARTNER:

- I've not been good at expressing what I need and I fear I'm burning out because if it. You may notice some changes in me speaking up more. I'm happy to talk about it, but just know I'm going to try to be clearer and more direct about what it is that I need.
- I love how you take care of me by _____. Would you be able to do that more often?
- I appreciate all you do to show me that you love me, but I feel the most loved when you _____.
- I'm noticing that I am getting irritated more easily. I know this means I need _____. How can we make that happen this week?
- Our schedule and all I'm carrying feels unsustainable. Let's set up a time to talk and find a better distribution.

TO YOURSELF:

- In this moment, what I need is _____.
- How can I shift my energy today to better meet one of my needs?
- What moments in my day allow for time or space to get a need met?
- How can I choose differently today so that I meet a need that I have?
- What can I let go of that will free up space/energy to meet one of my needs?

get a load of this

Personal Power

- What relationship-wrecking behaviors do you tend to resort to when you're in a difficult discussion?
- Can you identify what you're trying to protect yourself from or avoid?
- What's your replacement response so that this doesn't keep happening?

Better Together

Practice sharing a need you each have. Talk about whether this need requires something to be added, subtracted, or multiplied. Avoid relationship-wrecking behaviors when talking about this need.

CHAPTER
16

SHARE ACCOUNTABILITY

for us

Since becoming a parent, I'm often struck by the similarity between children and adults. In many ways, we still embody some of the same behaviors we're trying to parent out of our kids. If you don't know what I'm talking about, reflect on the last time you lost your cool. That's basically a grown-up tantrum. Were you hungry and grumpy? You probably felt like how your toddler feels when they're screaming for a snack. Were you tired and snapped at your kids? Maybe that's a little like your kid when they bit your head off after missing their second nap. Kids basically have the unfiltered and often socially inappropriate responses to things we still feel and want to express but don't because it's not okay. Inevitably, though, there will be times when we are so depleted that we cannot stay regulated, and during a moment of heightened emotions, we lose it or cross the line. Or we may never have learned to manage our emotions in a healthy way, only seeing adults in our life yell, rage, vent, blame, call names, or worse.

It's important to know that *how* you and your partner talk to each other is one of the most important factors in protecting your closeness and your relationship. If you engage in negative behaviors, it's time to own up to them and make a shift. If you keep your cool but display irritation in the form of rolled eyes or heavy sighs, I'm also talking to you. In this section, I will review some ways that you and your partner must take accountability for how you talk to each other.

There are two ways we communicate: with our words and with our body.

Verbal Communication

The words that we use are powerful and have the ability to build one another up or cut each other down. When couples haven't learned how to navigate tough conversations well, they easily can engage in below-the-belt behaviors. Here are some examples of negative phrases and behaviors in relationships:

- "You're just like your mom, nagging me all the time." (name calling and labeling)
- "You're a jerk." (insulting and belittling)
- "You *always* . . ." or "You *never* . . ." (overgeneralizing and exaggerating)
- Using the word "divorce" any time something gets heated (threatening and weaponizing)
- Attacking someone's character (character assassination)
- Yelling (verbal escalation)
- "Well, if you wouldn't have done X, I wouldn't have done Y." (blame shifting)

These communication tactics erode a sense of trust, security, and connection in your relationship. Ultimately, you're accountable for how you speak to your partner and how you react to your partner. You can get angry, but no one can *make* you say certain things or behave in a specific way. You must take accountability for how you show up and speak to each other.

What Getting It Right Looks Like

When it comes to healthy communication, most relationship professionals agree on what good communication looks like. I've already explained the relationship-wrecking responses, but what does it look like to get it right?

"Right" looks like a couple's ability to approach a conversation without worrying that the other person will dismiss or minimize their perspective. It looks like acknowledging the other person's perspective before jumping into your own. A very common skill used to accomplish this is called *restatement*.

I once watched a famous relationship duo practice this onstage and it felt like I was watching two parrots continually repeating back to each other what the other said. My high school self had to work overtime not to giggle during their keynote presentation. Restatements should *not* be parroting what your partner says but rather reflecting back to them that you heard, understood, and are absorbing their perspective.

When you get good at restatements, you take the conversation deeper, showing that you understand your partner, rather than switching the conversation to be about you and your perspective.

Here are a few rules about restatement:

1. **Before you react and respond, restate.** "So you're saying that when I didn't do X, you felt Y. I can really see how it would come across that way." Here are some starters to help you ease into this skill:
   » "What I'm hearing you say is . . ."
   » "You must have felt X when . . ."
   » "I can really see how when I did X, it had Y impact on you . . ."
   » "Let me make sure I'm hearing you accurately . . ."
2. **After you restate, ask for any edits from your partner.** "When I didn't call you to let you know that I was going to be home late, you felt like I didn't care about you or consider you. Am I getting this right?"

3. **When you restate, elaborate.** Usually when we are in a difficult conversation, we tend to explain our perspective in way more words than we use to explain our partner's. Try to restate their perspective by giving them the same amount of time and effort. Elaborate what you're hearing, get in their shoes, and then ask them if it feels reflective of their experience.

This relatively simple skill will dramatically increase feelings of being heard and understood in your conversations. It also has a side effect of slowing the pace of the conversation down, which will help keep things from getting heated quickly. As you work to improve your verbal communication, it's also important to be aware of how your body language comes across.

Nonverbal Communication

The second area of accountability around communication has to do with nonverbal communication. Nonverbal cues are how your body or tone conveys a message even when your words are saying something else. My dad and I came up with the term *crazy-making* that referred to the inconsistency between someone's words and their behavior. It's maddening because when it shows up, if you call it out, the person can just deny it and then flip the script, calling you "sensitive" or "crazy," when in actuality they are the ones who are engaging in poor and detrimental relationship behaviors. Here are some common negative behaviors when it comes to nonverbal communication:

- Sighing or visible irritation
- Looking at their phone when being spoken to
- Eye rolling
- Condescending laugh or smile
- Visibly distracted or acting uninterested
- Saying they're not mad but then acting mad or passive-aggressive
- Giving the silent treatment

- Storming off
- Throwing things, punching walls, or any type of aggression

When it comes to "right" nonverbal communication, it's important to show congruency between emotions, spoken words, and behavior and to engage in body language that shows receptivity to what your partner is saying.

Think about your body posture and positioning:

- Are you open and facing your partner?
- Are distractions put aside or away?
- Are you sitting down, giving your attention to the conversation?
- Are you listening or just reacting?

Work to become more aware of both your congruency and your body language.

One final note on nonverbals: There are specific nonverbals around the mental load that can drive partners crazy. For example, when a damp towel isn't hung up but rather tossed on the floor like you live in a luxury hotel and the maid will come clean it up, it communicates something. Now, I'm not saying you *intended* the message it communicates, but it's saying something nonetheless. Both partners have to be aware of the meaning they make of these nonverbals. Know that these gestures are communicating strongly whether you mean them to or not.

Rules of Engagement

An important step to having accountability in the way that you and your partner communicate is to develop a "rules of engagement" agreement for the acceptable and unacceptable ways you can communicate during difficult conversations. The benefit to having an agreement around your communication is that you can refer back to it if one of you strays from the agreed-upon rules.

RULES OF ENGAGEMENT AGREEMENT

We promise to avoid negative behaviors in our conversations, which include	
If we get into a tough spot during a discussion we will	
If one of us doesn't stick to our agreement, we will address it by	

Having these rules of engagement will hopefully minimize the number of times you and your partner have to apologize to each other for hurtful words or behavior, but also know that saying sorry is an important part of sharing accountability in your relationship.

Saying You're Sorry

If you're a parent, you've probably witnessed the forced, insincere apology. You tell your child to apologize, and they roll their eyes and breathe out an exaggerated "soooorrrry" steeped in attitude. Depending on what's going on, you either just let it go because you're exhausted from playing referee or you now have to tackle the attitude that ruined the apology.

Or maybe you subscribe to the "I won't make my kids apologize" camp. If that's you and your kids aren't taught the need to apologize, I want to encourage you to consider teaching your kids how to repair and take accountability for their actions or words. I totally get it, forcing a crap apology isn't really teaching much of a skill either, but learning how to take accountability for our choices is important—otherwise imagine what this kid will look like in adulthood. And maybe you don't have to because you're married to this type of apologizer (or lack of apologizer). Or maybe this is you. Apologizing can be really hard because it requires humility and the acknowledgment that you caused someone else pain, but it is an essential skill in lasting relationships. Here are a few things to consider about apologizing.

1. **Just because you didn't do something "wrong" doesn't mean you don't have to apologize.** I've sat with tons of adults who refuse to apologize because they "weren't wrong." Are they really arguing technicalities to avoid saying "I'm sorry" to a person they love? It's sort of silly. If you bump into someone in a hallway, would you say sorry? Of course you would, even if it was technically an accident. So the logic of "I only say sorry when I've done something wrong" (which is subjective) is flawed. Here are some examples of times you may need to say "I'm sorry":
   » When you've unintentionally hurt someone you love
   » When you have done something wrong
   » For the way you "came across," such as using a snappy tone or being distracted on your phone, which can feel invalidating or dismissive
2. **"I'm sorry you feel that way" isn't actually an apology.** This statement personally grates on me. This is an empty apology; why don't you just pepper in the eye roll and sassy tone? It's not demonstrating any real responsibility or accountability for one's part in the interaction.
3. **"Buts" aren't really that big of a deal.** This is a pet peeve of mine in the "relationship expert" space. Many experts say that "buts" don't have a place in an apology. I *sort of* agree, yet part of the reason people struggle to apologize for how they came across to their partner is because they likely have an explanation, and if they apologize, it seems like they are admitting fault without their perspective being considered. What matters is where you place the "but." If the "but" is placed *after* the apology, like "I'm sorry I forgot to pick up milk, but I was on a phone call with a work colleague and blah blah blah" then it feels like the "but" nullifies the "sorry" part and that the person really isn't that sorry. It sounds more like they feel justified in what happened. Consider

this phrase, however: "On the way home I got a stressful work call from a colleague and I totally forgot to pick up the milk, but I am so sorry. I know you needed that tonight." This apology feels way different. Try to use "but" to introduce the apology if you need to offer up an explanation.

4. **Learn to accept an apology.** In an apology, the receiver also plays an important role. If your partner apologizes and you just say, "Okay, whatever" or you are someone who likes to dig in with "Yeah, you should be sorry. You really ruined my night and hurt my feelings and so on and so on," then you have to work to actually *hear* and *believe* your partner's apology. Practice saying, "I accept your apology, thank you" when your partner humbles themselves in this way. Again, applying this stuff to your kids always offers a new perspective. If your kid said "whatever" to an apology, you'd probably intervene immediately.

5. **Have a formula for a good apology.** A good apology offers the words "I'm sorry" along with an elaboration of the offense. This helps the partner receiving the apology to feel understood and like their partner "gets it." This formula looks like this:

I'm sorry + What you're sorry for

Now, if you feel like you need to apologize for something but also offer up a rationale for why it happened, it may look like this:

I'm sorry + What for + Explanation + "But"
and a restatement of the apology

For example, "I'm so sorry for my snappy tone tonight. I feel so overwhelmed at home and at work, *but* I should not have taken that out on you. I'm really sorry."

Apologize often and freely in your relationship. As with most positive relationship behaviors, you aren't going to lose ground when you practice them—in fact, quite the opposite. You will enrich your relationship, help each other feel safe and loved, and it will help you grow in your connection.

get a load of this

Personal Power

Identify one verbal and nonverbal thing you do that could be sabotaging productive communication in your relationship.

Better Together

- Share the nonverbal or verbal communication pattern that is getting in the way of productive conversation with your partner and take accountability for it. Share how you will approach it differently next time.
- Take this opportunity to apologize to each other for either a negative verbal or nonverbal pattern that has hurt your partner in the past.

CHAPTER
17

SHARE ACCOUNTABILITY

for the mental load

A common predicament many women find themselves in is that they hand off a task to their partner and then their partner does the task but not to completion. This puts the woman in a very tricky and, quite honestly, crappy spot. Is she to remind her partner that he didn't finish the job—"Um, hey, when you clean the kitchen you also have to wipe down the counters"—which comes with feeling like a nag and possibly being perceived as a nag and ultimately may cause her to see her partner as an extra child and her partner to view her as the uptight mother? Neither of these personas is sexy.

Another option is that she mentions it and he responds with defensiveness: "Geez, your standards are so high." Or the deficit default. All sucky options. Or does she let it go and just bury her irritation? If you've ever heard your partner banging around the pots and pans (conveniently left soaking in the sink) or tossing around bath toys left in the tub, you may want to ask yourself if you actually completed the task. If she "lets it go," maybe she indeed has the ability to be okay with it, but over time, most women will start to develop resentment. So, which is it, nag or resentment? No thank you. I think I'd prefer personal accountability for $400, Trebek.

HER PERSPECTIVE

I do it all but my husband has opinions on how it should be done. How the kids should be raised. How the organizing should be done. How the cleaning should be done and when. But he won't do any of it. Won't give me input for dinner and then complains about what I make, so now I'm constantly looking for validation before cooking. I have no desire for intimacy with him and I struggle to even want to be around him or communicate because it seems to fall on deaf ears every time.

I feel frustrated and bitter and am critical, and then my partner walks on eggshells around me, which annoys me even more.

HIS PERSPECTIVE

Our sense of urgency is different. I definitely arrange my priorities with myself in mind, but my wife doesn't do this as much. It just feels like she pays the price for it. I wish she would care for herself more. I try to do what I can before she gets home from work (I work from home) so she can have a clear head, but it doesn't seem to do much.

Our home and its state isn't something I'm judged for but I know society holds women responsible for what a home looks like. I think that's made a major difference in how we have shaped our expectations.

There are two areas you and your partner must talk about when it comes to sharing accountability for tasks involved in the mental load: What's your "good enough" and what on-the-job training do you need?

What Does "Good Enough" Look Like?

As discussed earlier, you and your partner have expectations for each other that likely differ. The same applies to your expectations for tasks around the home. Not just what tasks are important, but also what doing a task well actually looks like. Maybe you really are invested in towels being folded a particular way but your partner isn't. You have to determine what good enough looks like for the two of you. Try to keep in mind that your investment in a particular task and how it's done may be very different from your partner's. Sometimes this will require a *leveling up* to do the task in this way, *letting go* to just abandon this standard all together, or *lightening up* to lessen the standards around a particular task.

I cannot give you the answer to what standards are reasonable and what are not; this is something you and your partner must negotiate on your own. However, the point is that you need to negotiate these things so that there is some agreed-upon standard of what is considered good enough.

Here's what I don't want you to do. I don't want you to get into a debate around why a particular standard or priority is "stupid" or a "waste of time." Again, this is just energy expended that will harm your relationship, not enhance it. So, ditch the judgment and work to establish what good enough looks like. I will help guide this conversation by defining what "good enough" is and then offering some guidelines for establishing your standards.

Good enough is

- done in a way that doesn't result in someone else having to re-do it,
- done to a standard that both partners can live with (not excessive and not sloppy), and
- done to completion.

Perhaps you've heard the saying "Done is better than perfect." While true, I realize there are certain tasks that may require more care and precision. When Roy was in preschool, they had a militaristic stance on tree nuts. I realize that some of you reading this may immediately feel defensive about peanut allergies, and I get it, that's serious business. I have a friend whose two kids will have violent and deadly allergic reactions, so I'm not making light of this. I want to be clear that this school's stance was not just about peanuts; it was about anything coming from a tree that could be considered a nut or that was made in a factory that produced anything that came from those trees.

I am not a perfectionist. I have high standards for certain things but I often do things quickly and sometimes sloppily. I don't always catch the fine print. And so I packed Roy's lunch with, what felt like to me, the precision of a retired Midwesterner pruning their bushes, but I cannot even tell you how many times I got a nastygram from his preschool about some obscure ingredient that they decided was off-limits. For Pete's sake (who is Pete anyway?), I was running out of things to pack.

The straw that broke this camel's back was when his cookies were sent home with a note attached. This one ticked me off because these cookies were a special treat he knew I packed and was looking forward to. The reason the cookies were designated contraband was that they were manufactured in a facility that may also handle coconuts, and coconuts are tree nuts. (I know who the real nuts were, and they weren't the cookies.)

My point is, some tasks require militaristic precision because there are consequences to getting it wrong. Like Roy not getting his cookies and other parts of his lunch. Or a kid at school with serious allergies being in danger. However, be aware of becoming so rigid around tasks that it puts your partner in a position where they feel like they're walking on eggshells about to get their next nastygram. Carefully consider what you want to have strict standards around. Revisit the Explore Your Expectations Exercise on page 123 to map out these expectations so you're on the same page. These can help you both to stay accountable to each other, and if someone doesn't hold up their end of the bargain, you have these agreements to refer back to. Also, please note you don't have to do this for everything in your home and family life. But I bet there are certain tasks that regularly cause tension or disagreements. Start there and then use this list as needed:

- What are some tasks that I feel strongly about being done in a particular way?
- What does "good enough" for these tasks look like?
- Why is this important?

The other part to this is determining what "done to completion" means. In *Fair Play*, Eve Rodsky has the concept of CPE, which stands for conception, planning, and execution. She states that when a person takes on a task, they should take it all the way from thinking it through to executing the task.[1] I think this is fantastic for so many couples; however, there are couples who prefer a more flexible approach. Perhaps you tag team a project or item. Or, like me, sometimes your partner isn't around to share in the task and sometimes they are.

So, consider how the two of you want to handle the division of a task. Is it 100 percent yours if you take it on, or do you share how the task is divided? Let's just call these *owned* and *shared* tasks. The owned tasks mean that one partner does the entire CPE; for example, my husband handles all things finances. This was something I turned over about eight years ago and have not thought about it since. It's 100 percent his.

Now, shared tasks are more flexible, like how our family handles vacations. Chad plans the entire thing, but I do all the prep work at home getting the house ready to leave, making sure the kids have clothes that fit and are worthy of going out in public, and I do all the packing (not for my husband, but for everyone else). Technically, this is a shared task. We will get into the nitty-gritty of this more in the next chapter, but consider this very important question: How will you and your partner hold each other accountable when one of you doesn't complete the task you agreed to take on or doesn't do it to the "good enough" standard? The fine print on this question is "without getting defensive, argumentative, or putting the other down."

Take a moment to come up with a strategy for how to hold each other accountable in these situations. Here are some ideas to get you started:

- If you're okay reminding, ask your partner for "permission to nag." I have a friend who shared this with me and I think it's such a quick and practical way to get permission quickly in the moment. This one isn't for everyone, but take into consideration the reality of relationships, which is that this stuff still happens even when you get good at sharing the load.
- Come up with a code word or phrase. When teaching our kids to honor each other's "stops," they came up with the phrase "pickle juice," which means STOP IMMEDIATELY. For some reason it worked better than a simple "stop." It was silly and defused defenses. The same can work for you and your partner.
- Agree to be open to feedback. Work to not interpret things as criticism but instead consider it helpful feedback that continues to propel your relationship forward. Remember the growth mindset; now's a good time to lean into it.
- You can use the three strikes approach, which is that you let it go two times before you bring it up. You have to know if you can handle this. But sometimes we forget things, life is busy and we drop a ball, or something comes up. This approach offers a boundary around your generosity so that you can both offer grace but also have a limit so that you don't build resentment or end up having to take another thing on.

If none of these sounds appealing to you, come up with your own plan.

When one of us doesn't complete a task to the "good enough" standard, we will handle it by	If one of us doesn't complete a task we took on, we will address it by

I want to remind you that the process of shifting the mental load is a long game. These changes take time to make and it's normal for there to be setbacks along the way. Be easy on each other and continue to push forward. Your effort and work will make a difference in your relationship.

On-the-Job Training

When you start a new job, you almost always receive some type of training that lets you know your responsibilities and what the expectations are of your performance. If you complete your training and then you can't ever remember what you need to do, you're going to get fired. When it comes to our relationships, know this:

- We may need some on-the-job training if the task is new and if there are specific standards around the task.
- We need to remember what we learned during the training so that we don't have to keep coming back to our partner and asking them each time. Having a partner who is helpless and requires hand-holding isn't attractive.
- We need to use our head. Even though I'm acknowledging that there may be some required training or new information when taking a task on that we didn't previously handle, please don't forget to use common sense and resourcefulness. Nothing is more frustrating than someone who is totally capable acting as if they are helpless.

You are responsible for seeking out the training you need for a specific task. In the story I told about Chad taking responsibility for the balloons for Roy's party, there were a lot of moving parts, but one natural solution would have been Chad taking initiative to ask me what I wanted for the balloons. He needed training, but if he didn't seek it out, I couldn't do anything to help and ultimately the job wasn't handled. You and your partner need to take accountability for asking for the training you need, and when your partner approaches you for this instruction, it's important you receive it with some level of understanding. The on-the-job training is part of collecting data because it helps to teach the steps and standards necessary to get it done and get it done to a "good enough" level.

get a load of this

Personal Power

- How flexible are you around what "good enough" looks like when it comes to the mental load? Do you need to increase flexibility at all?
- How defensive or combative are you when it comes to your partner's standards? Do you show some level of deference to hearing them out or do you push back, accusing them of making things too hard? Try to conduct an honest assessment of how you approach your partner's standards.

Better Together

Revisit some of the household responsibilities that may need to have their "good enough" standards tweaked. Is there any training necessary? Are there any conversations that need to be revisited?

PART
3

practically
speaking

CHAPTER
18

the handoff

I'm fun but I don't feel that way anymore," said Nina in our interview
on the mental load. This sentiment was echoed in different ways by
each of the women I interviewed. It makes me think of a character from
the show *Family Guy*, named Buzz Killington, who always enters the
scene and ruins it with his lameness. This feeling of "I used to be fun"
and "I feel like a buzzkill" is almost universal for women and a source
of resentment for sure. Part of the reason the resentment grows is that
women feel like they have to carry the weight of being the responsible
one, for moving the day forward, for setting the limits (because we
do the research), and for instituting structure, because it can feel like
no one will step up if we don't. One partner becomes Buzz Killington
and the other gets to be Free Willy. It doesn't feel fair, and feelings of
unfairness breed contempt, repulsion, and resentment.

The alternative that becomes a difference maker is sharing the
responsibility around the mental load so it feels like you're on the same
page. It becomes you both versus the world instead of you versus your
partner. This shift is a game changer. This chapter is going to cover an
essential task for navigating the mental load better as a couple. You've
already (hopefully) done the deep-dive work around the four areas

necessary to share (perspective, expectations, ownership, and account-ability); this is going to help you stay on top of those areas and to create a quick and manageable plan for making sure you don't find yourself in a bad place around the mental load moving forward.

Renegotiating Responsibilities

Have you ever thought about how many agreements are made in your relationship that you never actually talked about? Sometimes things shift through the years and one partner changes an agreement with-out even mentioning it to the other, and all of a sudden the dynamic changes. New expectations click into place and new disappointments likely follow. Roles and responsibilities are one major area of a relation-ship that is susceptible to these silent-agreement bombs that can blow up your relationship. Maybe it happened right off the bat, maybe things shifted after kids, but many have likely subscribed to agreements they've never discussed in their relationship that have one partner car-rying more of the mental load. If you don't know what I mean, think about how it was decided that you would be the one to buy presents for your partner's family, or that you would plan out holidays and magic-making for your kids, or that you would be the one coming up with dinner ideas. Did you actually talk about this?

Some of you will say yes, but the majority of you will not have had these conversations in your relationship. And if you said yes and are still reading this book, it means that it's not working for you. We touched on this in earlier chapters, but I want to reiterate again that we tend to fall into roles and carry responsibilities without much of a discussion. So, if you worry that you are nagging when you bring this up or that your partner will accuse you of beating a dead horse, I want you to hear me loud and clear: You've probably never negotiated. I mean *really* negotiated who does what in your relationship. You're not a nag or beating any horse to death; this is necessary for your relationship's health and survival. This is neces-sary for your well-being, and it's likely the first time you've actually had this conversation of really negotiating or renegotiating the roles and responsibilities in the home.

I'm going to give you some rapid-fire tips, some of which will be new and others will be reminders, for you to keep in mind as you have this discussion.

The Three Types of Support

Support comes in different forms. As you work through the negotiation, think about what types of support you can implement. You may feel like you need your partner to take on more, but sometimes what you may really need is for them to just acknowledge and appreciate all you do. Use the three A's discussed in chapter 14 to think about how you support each other around the mental load.

ASKING

- **Asking** can be asking what needs to be done.
  - » "What can I do to help you today?"
  - » "Is there anything I can take off your plate?"
  - » "What are some tasks that are feeling overwhelming that I can help with?"
  - » "I know _____ is coming up. What can I do to help prepare?"
- **Asking** can be asking how to do a task that is new for you so that you don't need to ask in the future.
  - » "I'd like to take XYZ off your plate, but I don't know how you'd like it done. Can you teach me?"
- **Asking** may be the default partner asking for what they need in order to make it visible to their partner. Here are some signs it may be time for you to speak up and ask for what you need.
  - » You're noticing a decrease in patience and are more irritable or easily set off by little things.
  - » You're taking things more personally or feeling pangs of resentment or frustration toward your partner or family.
  - » Your self-talk is sounding more like a victim. Do you feel like you're not being seen, appreciated, or validated?

ACTION

- **Action** can be shown through words that help someone take more action in their relationship.
  - » "Was there a time today you wished you had help but didn't?"
  - » "What is something you did today that I should have noticed but didn't?"
- **Action** can be shown through taking initiative and collecting data.
  - » "I've got dinner covered."
  - » "Go take a minute to yourself."
  - » "I will pick up the kids tomorrow."
  - » "I miss you and want to have a date with you. I've got it covered."
  - » "Summer is coming. Can we talk about the plan for camps?"
- **Action** can be shown through affection.
  - » A big hug to greet one another
  - » A longer kiss
  - » Words of affection
  - » Approaching vs. distancing when one partner is stressed

APPRECIATION

- **Appreciation** is shown through the ultimate compliment: Observation + How it positively enhances your life
- **Appreciation** can be shown through validating and empathetic statements.
  - » "You must be exhausted."
  - » "I can't believe all that you do."
- **Appreciation** can be shown through gestures.
  - » Leaving a note for your partner to find
  - » Picking up their favorite treat
  - » Anything that shows that you thought of them

The Three F's

The three F's were reviewed in chapter 14, but it's worth recalling them here because if you don't allow for these three F's, it can sabotage handing off more of the mental load.

LET YOUR PARTNER

- **Fail.** Remember, you've probably had more practice and you're likely "better" at it, but give your partner the space to fail without tons of criticism or feeling like they're walking on eggshells.
- **Figure it out.** If this task is new to your partner, it makes sense that they will need time to figure out how it's done. If you quantify the number of times you've done something, chances are you have had more practice.
- **Fine-tune.** You and your partner may not do things exactly the same way, and that's okay. There is more than one way to accomplish various tasks. Unless you've decided that this task can only be done in a particular way, back off and let your partner fine-tune on their own.

If Things Get Heated

Throughout the book, I've covered different tactics and offered tools and scripts for what to do when conversations get derailed. But here are a few quick tips to refer to if things start to get heated in this discussion.

TRY

- I'm feeling overwhelmed. Can we take a break and start again?
- I'm feeling really upset. What I am hearing you say is this _____. Can you clarify if I am understanding you correctly?
- Let's stop and make sure we are understanding each other. This is what I am hearing.
- Can you explain what you're hearing me say?
- I love you and I want to resolve this. What do you need from me in this moment?

- You should have known.
- You always . . .
- You never . . .
- Calm down.
- You're such a . . .
- You're too sensitive.
- I know that you think I'm . . .
- It's all in your head.
- You're just like your mother.
- Other people agree with me that you are . . .

The Handoff

The handoff conversation is one that hopefully really only needs to take place once. After that you will move to just having the SHARE Agenda where you will make tweaks in how you're both handling the mental load so that you make sure you both feel good about it.

The goal of the handoff is to increase the visibility of the invisible tasks and to have your partner step in to take more initiative as well as take more on. The previous chapters hopefully helped you enter into this conversation with a strong base of skills, insight into one another, and revision of potential issues that will detour this conversation into rocky terrain. Don't hesitate to return to those chapters if you find yourself in a tough spot.

There are minor and major ways of increasing visibility when it comes to the mental load. Remember, so many of the things you've been carrying are often out of your partner's awareness. I'm not justifying this but am merely saying that making the invisible visible becomes a major part of shifting the mental load.

Minor Handoff Strategies

1. **Prevention.** I realize you may think, *For the love. It's too late.* I get it, but I'd bet with every year your kids get older, extracurriculars get added, or something else changes and new tasks and

responsibilities get introduced into the rhythms of daily routine. Remember: The demand and intensity of the mental load are always changing. Because of this, be careful of taking new things on *without* having a conversation about them or making them visible. Remember the concept of piling on precedents: You take something on out of love or convenience and therefore it's removed from your partner's awareness or, worse yet, they were never aware of it in the first place. It becomes yours without discussion, without negotiation. Simply put, stop doing this. All new things get discussed. All new things are visible to both partners. Increase your awareness of these moments where you're pulled to take it on.

2. **Narration.** I realize you may sound like a crazy person, but narrating what you do is helpful with both your partner and kids. Most tasks of life require multiple steps, so share this with your family. Narrate what's involved. You don't need to talk to yourself all day, but there will be opportunities to speak out the invisible. I often relay what I did that day to my husband: "Hey, babe. I picked up your deodorant for you and made sure to restock the toilet paper." This serves a couple of purposes. First, now he's aware that these things get done and there isn't a magical deodorant leprechaun dropping things off in his bathroom drawer—it's me, taking care of him and doing things he now doesn't have to. This allows him to be aware that I did it, that it needs to be done, and it's not a promise that I will continue to do it. Now he will often say, "I am almost out of deodorant. Want me to grab it or are you going to the store?" There's no hostility or irritation, but he's also not assuming it's on my plate, which is nice. The second purpose is that it allows for an opportunity for a partner to express appreciation. He will also tell me, "I took care of the property tax bill," which gives me a chance to say thank you and that I'm so glad I don't have to think about it. More often than not we do things in the dark, never speak of them, keep a tally of all that we do, and then get irritated when our partner doesn't know it or express appreciation. So, get narrating—it really does help.

3. **Asking.** I covered this extensively in an earlier chapter, but I want to cover it again briefly. Asking can be a sensitive issue because it can seem like so much of the mental load is common sense. But asking is inviting your partner into what is invisible and in your mind and acts as a tool to help them move toward taking initiative. If you're starting to build resentment and irritation, please ask the following questions to see if it's time to increase your asking. If you respond yes to any of the questions, it's time to consider asking for the support you need.

CHECK-IN: DO I NEED TO ASK FOR SUPPORT?

- Am I noticing a decrease in my patience? Am I feeling more irritable or easily set off by little things?
- Am I taking things more personally or feeling pangs of resentment or frustration toward my partner or family?
- Is my self-talk sounding more like a victim? Do I feel like I'm not being seen, appreciated, or validated?

Major Handoff Strategies

The biggest handoff strategy is to actually look through who does what and renegotiate. I'm a practical gal, so when my husband and I revisited our responsibilities, I knew I needed to hand over finances—and I mean *all* the things related to finances, including calling about bills when they don't make sense, paying them, and managing the budget. I didn't need to evaluate all we do; I just needed this behemoth task off my plate. I'm telling you this because there are all sorts of variations to what you and your partner need when it comes to the handoff. You may need to simply shift a few items or you may need the major overhaul. If it's simply shifting a few items, I think you can handle that on your own. But continue reading for some tips to implement along the way.

As I was writing this book, I was lucky to have a Zoom call with Eve Rodsky, author of *Fair Play*. I told her there's just no better solution for the actual handoff of tasks than the one she provides. And

I truly mean that. Eve Rodsky has a great resource called Fair Play cards, which can be divided up to see what each of you do. Then you renegotiate the cards so that they feel fairer. Remember, the goal isn't fifty-fifty; the goal is for the distribution of things to feel fair and for the burden between partners to be relatively comparable.

I have created a Mental Load List with items that are involved in the mental load that you can download using the Additional Resources QR code, or you can try the Fair Play cards. The list is in a spreadsheet format so you can edit and add to it as much as you'd like. As you work through this list, you can look at who does what and what you'd like to revisit. Make sure that as you work through the list and hand off an item, you discuss the following:

1. The standards for this task
2. What "good enough" looks like
3. What on-the-job training may be necessary

When you and your partner start to review this list, you have three options for how to handle a task.

1. **Divvy it up differently:** This means that the task transfers to the other partner.
2. **Delegate it:** This means that you involve someone else or hire it out. This can be things like having your kids take some responsibility or bringing in outside help. I realize that this depends on your budget and financial situation. Discuss these things together. There is no room for guilt if you're feeling like you should be able to do it all. One cheap way to get help is by ordering groceries online. Make sure to discuss who will manage this help, because that's a job too.
3. **Drop it:** Tasks can be dropped for a season or altogether. Sometimes our standards do need to lighten up and we can agree together (that's key) that a particular task can be eliminated from the list for now or for good.

IDEAS FOR TASKS TO HIRE OUT

- Washing or folding laundry
- Regular cleaning of your house
- Periodic or deep cleaning (e.g., refrigerator, sheets, bathrooms)
- Washing windows
- Gutter cleaning
- Meal prep or meal delivery service
- Online grocery order
- Dog walker
- Dog groomer, bather
- Babysitter
- Car washer
- Gardener
- Running errands (hire a student to pick up dry cleaning, go to Target, etc.)
- Tutor to help kids with homework
- Handyman for odds and ends around the house
- Professional organizer
- Carpet cleaner
- School transportation
- Hanging holiday lights

RESOURCES THAT CAN HELP

- Prime Now
- Instacart
- Shipt
- Taskrabbit
- Care.com
- Angi (formerly Angie's List)
- Thumbtack
- Facebook groups

When you renegotiate the mental load, think about each task and consider what you each like to do and what you are good at. I once heard someone tell a story about how her husband found a babysitter. It was a task she had always taken on herself but this time she asked him to figure it out. Well, her husband found a sitter Russian-roulette-style, sending a group text to all the sitters, and the first one to reply got the job. Not only did it work out great, but it was more efficient. He was better at it.

My husband is in charge of all things trash. I either chuck cardboard boxes off our deck toward the trash can or throw them, fully intact, into the bin and never think about them again. He will go out there on Sunday night with a razor blade and cut those suckers into snowflake-sized pieces. It takes forever. I'm sure it's therapeutic and gives him some time by himself, but he likes to do it and he's good at it. I don't care about the boxes, I move fast, I am sloppy with things like that, and I won't take the extra step to maximize space in recycling. It would make no sense for this to be my task.

Keep these things in mind as you and your partner renegotiate tasks. Allow for opportunities for your partner to surprise you when it comes to different tasks. They may have a better and more efficient approach, so be open to it.

I'll summarize this conversation in the chart on the next page. You may have different starting places depending on whether your partner is invested in this conversation, has read this book, or has some knowledge of what the mental load is.

Remember, it's the two of you against the world. In order to make this shift, you and your partner have to have a plan for regularly discussing the mental load without it turning into a big ordeal each time. When you share this responsibility for talking about the mental load and being invested and involved in it, one partner doesn't shoulder the burden alone. This creates the feeling of teamwork or togetherness around something that feels like such a barrier to closeness and connection in your relationship. Remember that women want reliable partners and men want more peace; both of these needs can be met when you have a sustainable plan for regularly checking in about the mental load. The next chapter will offer you this plan.

HANDING OFF THE MENTAL LOAD:
CONVERSATION PROMPTS AND SCRIPTS

Steps	Scripts and Strategies
1. Introduce the conversation.	"I would like to talk to you about something really important to me. When is a good time?"
2. Identify the problem.	"As you probably have noticed, I've been really overwhelmed. Lately and for a while. It is starting to interfere with my (insert here) and impact (insert here)." • "It's starting to interfere with my ability to enjoy life and I worry it is causing me anxiety that I didn't previously have." • "It is starting to interfere with my ability to get in the mood for sex and impact my headspace. I just can't ever seem to relax."
3. Introduce the concept.	"It's something that has a name because it is almost a universally shared experience of women. It is called the mental load and it is an invisible running to-do list that I carry with me at all times. It involves the physical tasks, mental tasks, but also the emotional tasks of life. [Try to give an example.] This never-ending list occupies a ton of space in my mind and I'd like to talk to you about shifting a few things so I can start to feel less overwhelmed and more like we're on the same page."
4. Turn down the heat (if necessary).	"This isn't a conversation about blame; it's me letting you into my internal experience and giving you insight into what is up with me so that we can work together to navigate this differently. Because I can't continue carrying this load in the same way."
5. Set a time to renegotiate.	"I'd like to set up a time to talk about this and work through some of the tasks. When is a good time?" (If you already feel confident and comfortable with numbers one through four, you can start here.)
6. Identify who does what/ tasks for handing off.	You can use the Fair Play cards or the download I've provided and work through identifying who does what. If this is an easy decision and you know exactly what you want to hand off, ditch the lists and go from there.

7. Determine the plan.	Use the three D's: delegate, divvy up, and drop. Consider what you are good at and what you like to do, to determine how the tasks are handled. Make sure that if you hand something new to your partner, you determine 1. the standards for this task, 2. what "good enough" looks like, and 3. what on-the-job training may be necessary.
8. Schedule your mental load meeting.	End the conversation reviewing your plan, expressing appreciation to each other, and setting a time for your regular mental load meeting. You can introduce the concept like this: "I realize that some of this is new and that life involves a lot of moving parts and pieces. Naturally the things we have to take care of as a family will continue to shift, so I'd like for us to have a regular [weekly is best] meeting to touch base with each other around the mental load. This way it's off my plate and we share it. I'll feel like more of a team with you. I also feel like then I won't carry anxiety about whether or not you'll check in with me; this will just be scheduled. If we have to revisit how we worked through these items, we can do it then. How does that sound?"

CHAPTER
19

your SHARE meeting

Scheduled Home and Relationship Effort

The most powerful thing you can do for your overall relationship and how you and your partner handle the mental load is to have regularly scheduled meetings to discuss who does what and where you each may need more support. I realize this may take some convincing, but trust me when I say it's worth it.

1. **When you have regular meetings about the mental load, you're tackling it as a team.** We've established that women tend to be the ones carrying the bulk of the mental load of the home and family. Of course there are exceptions, but for the most part, this is the norm. Because of this, women often feel lonely buried under the weight of it all. When resentment is piqued and she's feeling overwhelmed, naturally this tension starts to infiltrate the relationship, and before you know it, she's irritated with you and the overall tone in your relationship has soured. The main reason is that she feels alone. Where is her partner? The one who made promises to her. Not just a helper

but a partner. When you both make the decision to step into having regular meetings about the relationship, she will not feel as alone and you will not be the villain; instead the villain becomes the mental load and you two are working together to tackle it as a team.

2. **When you have regular meetings about the mental load, it takes things off her.** Women carry the emotional weight of the relationship: "Are we okay? Do we need a date? I need to tell him I'm upset about this or that but it's never a good time." This worry takes up so much space in the mental load. If you add kids into the mix, she is worrying about them, too, and their experiences and schedules and well-being. Furthermore, if she's handed something off, she may be worrying about whether or not it will actually get done. Having these regular meetings will naturally involve her partner in the relationship process. Just this simple shift will make a dramatic change in the relationship.

3. **Having a regular meeting saves you both from just down-loading information to each other.** When life gets really busy, more and more of your conversations start to focus around the logistics of life. Interactions become transactional. No more "What's your favorite memory growing up?" and other get-to-know-you conversations, but rather conversations about grocery shopping, kids' sports schedules, school pickups and permission slips, and so on. What also happens is that these download conversations are scattered through the week and likely happening in passing moments. This makes it easier for miscommunication to happen or information to get lost in translation: "You never told me that" followed up by "Yes, I did, ugh." Instead, have one meeting a week. Consolidate this conversation and spend the rest of the week enjoying each other. Boom.

4. **Having regular meetings helps you get amazing at talking about your relationship.** This may be the biggest benefit because, as I mentioned earlier, so many couples struggle with the idea that relationships actually take work and regular maintenance. But if you think about anything else in life, almost

nothing is "set it and forget it," yet we treat our most important relationship that way. The more you schedule these meetings, the better you'll get at them and the closer your relationship will become. Small issues won't build into major resentments. You will meet each other's needs better, be able to support each other in meaningful ways, know one another better, feel less stressed and more connected, and likely will have more and better sex. Are you in or are you in?

The first time Chad and I had a relationship meeting, we were at my parents' house. We went outside by a fireplace, had a glass of wine, and had what I thought was an amazing discussion. I felt closer and more connected. The next day, I told Chad that I loved our talk the previous night. He responded, "Are you kidding me? We fought the entire time." It's funny and not that funny at the same time. It's wild how perspectives can be so different. I say this to remind you that there are different levels of tolerance for these types of discussions, so make sure your mindset is in a good place. Here are some guidelines for this SHARE.

1. **Keep it positive.** Try to really practice your good communication skills. Take accountability for how you speak to each other (revisit the relationship-wrecking responses from chapter 15, if needed) and try to keep this meeting positive. Especially the first one, because you *want* to want to do it again.

2. **Keep it short.** Try to keep the meeting to around twenty minutes or less after the initial renegotiation. If the meeting drags on and you have deeper things to talk about, schedule another time to talk. If you go too long, you may just find yourself in the weeds talking about things that aren't necessary or that get you off track.

3. **If needed, get moving.** I've found that regular relationship talks can be tricky for men in particular. Something about the intensity of the face-to-face conversation can immediately stir

up discomfort. If necessary, try going on a walk together when you have this conversation or doing something where you're alongside one another versus staring at each other. Having an enjoyable ritual that involves movement attached to your SHARE meeting can go a long way in making sure it actually happens.

4. **Use an agenda.** I've provided an agenda or you can make your own, but most relationship habits that are new require that you're mechanical at first before you become more automatic. Don't treat this as a choose-your-own-adventure and just wing it. You will either go down a path you didn't intend to or you will sit there awkwardly staring at each other. It's already awkward when doing something new, so use an agenda to guide the conversation and then become looser with it as you get more skilled.

5. **Always schedule your next meeting.** Always put your next meeting on the calendar. If you just leave it up in the air, months may go by before it happens again. Or the default partner will be stressing about having to manage this as well. This meeting is critical because the mental load is constantly changing. If you want it to shift, you have to do this check-in.

Okay, let's do this. If you want to have a hard copy to write out notes or your own questions, you can print a SHARE Agenda using the QR code in Additional Resources.

SHARE Agenda

Questions to Discuss

- On a scale of 1 to 10, 1 being "Light" and 10 being "Unbearable," how heavy has the mental load felt this past week?
- On a scale of 1 to 10, 1 being "Fair" and 10 being "Not at all fair," how fair has the mental load felt this past week?

Share Perspective

- What perspective do you wish I had about you this week?
- What perspective would help me see you more accurately this week?
- Anything I could improve to be more on PAR (*pursuit, appreciation, reliability* for women, or *peace, affection, respect* for men)?

Share Expectations

- What expectations do you have for this coming week?
- Any expectations that went unmet last week?
- Any expectations that need to be leveled up, let go of, or lightened up?
- Do you need to rewrite the story you're telling yourself about me? Or about yourself?

Share Ownership

- How have we been taking more initiative? How have we been speaking up about what we need?
- What ownership needs to be taken around asking, action, or appreciation?
- What data have you collected this week?

Share Accountability

- How are we showing up in our relationship this week? Do I need to offer you any information about this (e.g., "I'm stressed about an upcoming deadline")?
- How are we speaking to one another? Do we owe each other an apology?
- Are things being done to our agreed-upon "good enough" standards? Is there any training necessary?

What Tasks Need to Be Discussed For the Upcoming Week?

- Divvy up
- Delegate
- Drop

> **Check In on Your Sex Life**
>
> - How is our overall feeling of closeness this week? What's one goal to increase feelings of security and love?
> - How connected is our sexual relationship this week? What's one goal we have for this week to enhance our sexual relationship?
> - What is one goal for our relationship this week?

There it is, folks. I believe that when you do this, your relationship will dramatically change. Please note that you can edit the questions as necessary and cover the ones that are relevant and skip those that don't fit. But this will keep you on track and address the major topics during your meeting.

You may have noticed a check-in for your sexual relationship. You must know that even if you've reached a better place with the mental load, if your sexual relationship struggled because of it, it may be a challenge to break out of your rut. If this is you or if you're still feeling disconnected in your sexual relationship, the next chapter is for you.

CHAPTER
20

a plan for a great sex life

A 2007 Pew Research report looked at factors that contribute to a happy marriage and listed them in this order:

1. Faithfulness
2. Happy sexual relationship
3. Sharing household chores[1]

Hopefully you're getting the picture that there's a relationship between the mental load and your sexual connection in your marriage. Before we get into a plan for your sex life, I want to call a few things out.

1. **Relieving the mental load will help, but don't do things looking for payment.** I cannot tell you how many times I've heard from women who say their husband cleans the kitchen and then expects sex. If your relationship is in a good place, maybe this is funny or cute. But for the majority of women, this will feel manipulative and like her partner is only doing things

for sex, rather than because he wants to take care of her. It feels, at the heart of it, rather self-serving.

2. **It makes sense if you or your partner want more sex.** Wanting more sex isn't a bad thing. It doesn't mean you or your partner care only about sex, but that it's likely part of how you feel connected and close. Throughout the course of relationships, it makes sense that your sex life will change. There are peaks and valleys, and if you're in a valley, it's understandable for you to wonder how you got here. To have a vibrant sexual relationship likely means you feel desired and connected; it makes sense to want more (or better) sex. If you're in a sexual dry spell, please know that this process may take some time to rebuild and it's important to be patient and honor your partner along the way.

3. **Sex starts outside the bedroom.** Sex is not just what happens between the sheets (or wherever else you prefer). It is what happens in your relationship all the time. If you come home from work irritated and snappy and sit at the counter on your phone or laptop all night, barely acknowledging your partner's presence, don't expect your partner to be raring to go come bedtime. It's just common sense. Weirdly enough, people often ignore things that are common sense. But if you've been paying attention, you'll know that feeling safe, secure, and loved in a relationship are paramount. If these things don't exist, or are struggling, it makes sense that desire will struggle too.

4. **Don't treat sex as a chore.** Sex is supposed to be enjoyable for both people involved. If you view sex as another item on your list that you have to tick off, it starts to feel like a chore, like something you do *for* your partner instead of *with* your partner. When you start to do things *for* another person, you're setting them or the situation up for eventual resentment. It starts to feel like just an obligation and like you aren't fully a participant in the process, like something that just takes from you and demands more from you. It is important that you check yourself and whether or not you subscribe to this mindset. Now, I get

it. I am a busy mom who understands that there will be times you're maybe checking a box. This goes for both of you. But if this is your norm and enjoying sex is actually the exception, it's time to shift your mindset because this way of thinking will cause issues in your sex life and irritation toward your partner.

5. **Fighting over frequency is common.** One of the most common disagreements around sex is regarding how much of it you're having. Usually one person wants more of it and the other person is happy where they're at or wants less. I say this to you because it feels good to have a gauge around where you and your partner stand in your sexual relationship. When couples struggle in relationships, it's often in silence, so it feels like you're the only ones dealing with an issue. But you aren't, not even a chance. If you and your partner have an equal desire, good for you! But if you don't, you're in the majority.

Many couples are curious about how much sex is the right amount. I hate to serve up the lamest answer, but here it is: The right amount of sex is whatever you and your partner both feel relatively good about. There's often a bit of compromise for both partners when it comes to their sexual relationship, but ultimately it has to feel good to both of you. If once a year is good, then great. If every day feels good to you both, enjoy! Just like with the mental load, there isn't a magical number here; it just has to feel relatively fair.

Sex Ed 101

Before we get into the plan for your sexual relationship, I need to explain some basic concepts about sex and how desire works. The reason this is so critical is that there are so many misunderstandings about desire that it's absolute bananas, and these misunderstandings can cause major disconnects in your relationship. If you want to delve deeper into some books on desire and your sexual relationship, I've compiled my favorites—just scan the Additional Resources QR code for my Sex Ed 101 book recommendations.

Are you in the mood?

Let's talk about desire or libido. Desire is basically how in the mood you are for sex. I am going to explain how our desire works and two primary forms of desire. This part is important because if you don't understand it, you may feel really crappy about your level of desire or really unwanted by your partner because of their lack of desire.

The most widely accepted theory of desire is called the Dual Control Model of Sexual Response developed by Dr. John Bancroft and Dr. Erick Janssen in the late 1990s.[2] This theory states there are two separate systems involved in desire. The "go" system is the sexual excitatory system (SES), which you can think of as the accelerator of sexual desire. The SES is regularly scanning for things that are sexually relevant and that turn you on. If you're rolling your eyes thinking, *Oh, this is why my partner thinks any long hug is an invitation to get naked,* this hug is perhaps an activation of their SES. When the SES is activated, all systems are go and desire is revved. The "stop" system, or the sexual inhibitory system (SIS), is the brake pedal. This system scans for things that are threatening or unsafe, and when it's detected, desire is shut down. These are the things that turn you off. Each system scans for signs to hit the accelerator or slam on the brake.

The systems operate independently and have different levels of sensitivity. Therefore, each person has a different combination of how sensitive their brake and their accelerator are. Maybe you have a very sensitive accelerator (aka a cool breeze turns you on) but also a sensitive brake. (The cool breeze turns you on, but it smells weird so that turns you off.) The brake, unfortunately, tends to be more powerful than the accelerator.

Take a moment and consider where you fall in terms of sensitivity for both your accelerator and your brake—and also where your partner falls.

How sensitive is your accelerator?

Not much turns me on   Everything turns me on

I have so many turn-offs   Not much turns me off

How sensitive is your brake?

What things cause you to brake? What are the things that rev your engine and hit the accelerator? The goal for optimizing desire is to minimize all the things that hit the brake and maximize the things that hit the accelerator. Remember, the brake can overpower the accelerator. Therefore, if you're lying in bed, overwhelmed with all that's on your plate and angry because you asked for your partner to step up and the response was the deficit default, you're likely just riding that brake. Remember, for women especially, to be turned on, your brain has to be turned off (or at least the volume turned down).

What type of desire do you have?

It's wild how movies depict sex scenes—talk about setting people up for majorly unmet expectations. I mean seriously, can we all agree that no one is enjoying sex up against a wall with the woman suspended in air? It's just not happening. His biceps would be cramping and her hamstrings would be locked up. Ridiculous. Yet, these are the scenes we see over and over again on television shows or in the movies. These visual depictions of ravenous desire can leave us feeling like something is wrong with us or with our partner. This is why understanding what type of desire you have is key to having a mutually fulfilling sex life and taking ownership over this part of your relationship.

There are two types of desire:

1. **Spontaneous.** Spontaneous desire is what is portrayed most in movies. It's the type of desire that doesn't require a ton of intimacy to lead up to it and it can come out of nowhere. Around 75 percent of men have spontaneous desire compared to around 15 percent of women.[3] Here's the rub: This type of desire is often considered "ideal," so if you fall outside of this type you may wonder what is wrong with you. Nothing! Nothing is wrong with you—you just may have the other type of desire.

2. **Responsive.** Responsive desire almost always requires participation in order to feel aroused. Let me say it again: Arousal follows participation. It's estimated that about 30 percent of

women have responsive desire as opposed to 5 percent of men.[4] My husband and I joke that whenever we have sex (even if we were tired at the start), it's never a bad idea. For me, someone who is responsive in my desire, I have to recognize that I may not *feel* in the mood very often, but if I participate I will *get* in the mood. I'm hoping that this simple piece of information clears up some major issues in your sex life. If you feel like you should be in the mood more than you are, maybe you just have responsive desire. If your partner feels like you should be in the mood more, maybe they need to understand the difference between these two types.

An important takeaway from responsive versus spontaneous desire is that if you're the one with the responsive desire, you may have to decide to participate before you feel ready, because if you wait for your arousal to occur before you participate, you and your partner may never have sex.

I realize there's more to this because sex starts outside the bedroom, but this is a really crucial step in taking some ownership over your sexual relationship. Your partner may need to create better conditions for you to feel sexually safe and you may need to be willing to participate to stir up arousal.

If you read all of this but think that something else may be going on with your or your partner's desire, review the Low Libido Checklist. This can help you and/or your partner explore other alternatives with your medical or psychological professionals. Please note that talking about some of these things, especially for men, can feel very vulnerable and uncomfortable. I mentioned it in a previous chapter, but just like there's a socialization around sex for women, there is for men too. They're supposed to be ready to go all the time and have sexual prowess and vigor. If they don't, it can feel emasculating, which can unfortunately cause a lot of men to not talk about something that's very important. When considering reasons for your lower desire, here are general categories to think about with some examples (the list is not exhaustive).

LOW LIBIDO CHECKLIST

- **Physical symptoms:** stress, chronic pain, hormonal issues, underactive thyroid
- **Medication use:** SSRIs, beta blockers, antihistamines
- **Psychological reasons:** sexual abuse, internalized messages about sex
- **Relational issues:** resentment, trust issues or betrayal, unmet needs
- **Extra-marital:** pornography use, affairs

Where does closeness fit in?

My husband travels for work, and if he's been gone for more than a few days, we both feel disconnected upon his return. He acts sort of strange around me until we have sex. Sex is his bridge back to me. He feels loved and safe with me when our sexual relationship is strong. If it weren't strong, he'd feel unwanted by me (in all ways). Understanding that sex is relational for many people is important when it comes to your mentality around sex. Instead, sex is too often considered primal or animalistic or even unnecessary. Like "Hey, all your needs are met in every stinking way, but you need this too? What's your deal?" Again, it can too often be thought of as an unnecessary part of a relationship by the person with lower desire or a cherry on top instead of a necessary ingredient. Instead of thinking of sex in this way, think about what sex means to each of you in reference to your relationship closeness. Speaking generally, for most men sex makes them feel loved and is necessary for closeness; for most women, feeling loved and close is necessary to be in the mood and feel safe having sex.

What role does sex play?

Closeness   Sex

Sex   Closeness

Thinking about this for yourself and then discussing it with your partner can help shift your understanding around your sex life and the important role it plays. If you're someone who thinks closeness is necessary for getting in the mood for sex, but your partner has said they will never meet your needs, there is no way you'd really want to have sex with them. The reverse works too: If your partner needs sex to feel close and you're asking for them to meet your needs in a new way, but you've taken sex off the table, they may feel less close and safe to do so.

The Sexual Standoff

A very common dynamic that occurs in a couple's sex life is the sexual standoff. This dynamic easily and often develops around the mental load. When the partner who desires more participation in the home and family life isn't getting what they want, they start to withdraw; when the partner who wants more intimacy isn't getting it, they start to withdraw. This leaves a couple at a standoff because both partners are not getting their needs met, and then they hold out, can't access desire to be intimate or care about their partner's needs, or are stingy about giving their partner what they want. In essence, each partner won't give until they get.

What happens is that partners can get really entrenched in this pattern to the point where they don't really even remember what started it, but they both end up so angry at each other and disconnected that it's difficult to know where to begin. It can feel hopeless and lonely. This also leaves your relationship vulnerable to affairs, porn use, and other types of infidelity. I do not say this to stir up more anxiety or fear, but rather to say that this is serious and can cause significant damage to a relationship. I'm also not saying that the men will run off and have the affair. Recent data has shown that around 70 percent of all divorces are initiated by women, and when you look at college-educated women, it's around 90 percent.[5] Both partners are at risk in this situation.

The difficult part of resolving it is that one partner has to step toward the other. I asked you at the beginning of this book to approach your relationship with humility. It's time to put your money where your mouth is because humility in this area can feel really difficult. One partner has to humble themselves enough to initiate care of their partner, to end the standoff, and to start to rebuild connection in a new way.

A Problematic Pattern

Another common pattern that can develop for couples who don't have the same desire (which is most couples) is that the partner with the higher desire is always looking for the green light, which means nearly all types of touch spark a bit of hope that sex is right around the corner. What can happen is that the partner with the lower desire picks up on this and starts to avoid touch altogether in order to not send the wrong message. If they kiss and the kiss extends a bit longer than usual, the higher-desire partner will potentially expect sex, and so the lower-desire partner starts to cut those kisses short. Or hug less. Or smack a butt less. Or even recoil at their partner's touch. Emotionally, the lower-desire partner may start to feel like their partner only touches them when they want sex. The higher-desire partner will start to miss out on the touch from their partner and this will create feelings of insecurity and feeling unwanted. I want you to be aware of this pattern, because if you're here, you may have to do some communicating around how you can get in the habit of touching more and kissing more in your relationship without it leading to sex. Practicing regular no-strings-attached touch will rewire this dynamic and increase the closeness in your relationship.

A Plan for Your Sexual Relationship

It blows my mind how uncomfortable couples feel talking about sex. You'll get naked and do the thing but talking about it, what are you crazy?! In this section, I want to encourage you to have five key conversations about sex that can help you and your partner resurrect this area of your relationship if it's been struggling, or enhance your sexual relationship if you're doing okay in this area. Please note that this isn't something that needs to be done often. If you find yourself in a sexual rut, then by all means, revisit these questions. However, for the most part, you may need to do this once in your relationship and then, moving forward, just use the check-in question I provided on your SHARE Agenda.

Remember, sex is a sensitive topic in relationships. It's critical that you and your partner engage in these conversations with the goal of caring for each other and ultimately working toward a more mutually fulfilling sex life. These conversations are intended to help you explore topics that you may have felt too uncomfortable to discuss or didn't know how to initiate. If at any point a history of trauma, abuse, or any triggering episode comes up, please consider bringing this to a professional to help you navigate this sensitive subject.

Conversation 1: What turns you on? What turns you off?

When it comes to sex, people will most often talk about or think about the things that turn them on. This is great, but if you remember from earlier, it is only one piece of the puzzle. Our brakes play a major role in desire. So take some time and really discuss the things that both hit your brakes and your accelerator.

Ask yourself, what are the perfect conditions for getting in a sexy state of mind? Just in case you need some nudging, turn-ons can be anything. For example, my husband wore Cool Water cologne when we first met. The smell transports me to the early years in our relationship and does it for me. In fact, good smells hit my accelerator, but a gross smell and you're dead to me. I dropped hints for years about that cologne and finally I had to say outright, "Order the dang cologne—you don't know what you're missing." And he did. And it made a difference. Remember, both brakes and accelerators can be sexual and nonsexual things (because sex starts outside the bedroom). Take a second to think about what hits your accelerator (aka what turns you on) and what hits your brake (aka what turns you off).

Also, include in this conversation how sensitive both your brakes and accelerators are, because this matters. Keep in mind you want to maximize what hits the accelerator and minimize what hits the brakes.

How sensitive is your accelerator?

Not much turns me on   Everything turns me on

|————————————————————|————————————————————|

I have so many turn-offs   Not much turns me off

How sensitive is your brake?

Follow-up question: What's something you've always wanted to incorporate in your sexual relationship or fantasized about?

Conversation 2: What does sex mean to you?

I explained the importance of this differentiation already, but this conversation can be a game changer for you and your partner and how you think about your sex life. Understanding how you and your partner attribute meaning to your sexual relationship is important to understanding the lens through which you both view this part of your relationship.

I recommend couples ask each other these four questions to explore this aspect of their sexual relationship:

1. What does our sexual relationship mean to you? What do you feel it adds to our relationship?
2. If we aren't having as much sex as you'd like, what conclusions do you draw about our relationship?
3. If we aren't having as much sex as you'd like, how do you imagine I feel about you?
4. When we are having sex as often as you'd like, how do you imagine I feel about you?

Conversation 3: I find you sexy when . . .

When there is a disconnect in your sexual relationship, one or both of you may feel unwanted or undesired. This conversation will help you focus on the aspects of your partner that you love, appreciate, and find sexy. Additionally, it helps you and your partner understand what things contribute to you both getting in a sexy state of mind. You may be surprised at the things that your partner finds sexy about you and vice versa.

Here are some prompts to get you started:

- You are most sexy to me when . . .
- I love when you wear . . .
- One of the things I appreciate most about you is . . .
- I get turned on by you when you . . .
- You bring me the most pleasure when you . . .
- I've never told you this before but I love when you . . .
- I feel most loved by you when . . .

Conversation 4: Spontaneous vs. Scheduled

This conversation and strategy can be one of your best to getting out of a sexual rut—if you can get over any hang-ups you may feel about scheduling sex. I suppose the ideal vision of a healthy sexual relationship is one where couples want each other all the time, yet this isn't the reality for most people. So, when life hits and you find yourself having sex less and less, consider incorporating some scheduled sex into your routine if spontaneous sex isn't working. Part of the reason why this is so key is that when a couple is in a sexual funk, usually one partner has been initiating more than the other. If this partner continues to get turned down, they will stop initiating. If the other partner never really initiated, and the regular initiator has stopped, then you have a relationship that becomes sexless or close to it. This is fine, if you're both on board with this, but I'd venture a guess that the one who has stopped initiating feels dejected and unwanted. Asking them to step into initiating again to get back on track is too vulnerable for many, which is where scheduling comes in.

Scheduling sex helps in these ways:

1. It takes the pressure off initiating. You know it's going to happen, so it's just on.
2. It helps partners build anticipation throughout the day thinking about what's to come later (great for responsive desire).
3. It helps to ensure that you have sex, helping to bring the rut to an end.

I'm not saying you *must* schedule sex. If spontaneous is working for you, keep going. But don't underestimate this majorly helpful tool. Here are some questions to explore this aspect of your relationship.

- How do you feel about scheduling sex? If you're on board, let's set some dates.
- If we don't schedule, how often do you think it will happen spontaneously?
- If we decide to schedule, how often do you want to put it on the calendar?
- Are you up for a trial period of scheduling sex and revisiting it in three or four months?

Conversation 5: Who initiates?

Initiating sex is an act of vulnerability. Typically one partner takes the lead in this role. However, what can happen is that over time if this partner is repeatedly turned down, they may stop initiating. This can lead to them feeling hurt and shutting down, withdrawing, or the other person being confused as to why their partner doesn't initiate anymore.

Another common pattern is that one partner initiates but when their partner isn't a yes they pout or make comments that hurt their partner. This can happen even when they have a relatively healthy sexual relationship. This makes the partner who isn't initiating feel like they're either stuck saying yes when they don't want to or that they have to deal with the attitude and judgment that will come from their partner if they say no.

A final pattern is that the partner who initiates can begin to feel unwanted if their partner doesn't show an interest toward them. Hopefully understanding responsive and spontaneous desire can help battle this feeling, but it makes sense that over time feelings of hurt or confusion as to why they aren't being pursued come into play. Having a frank discussion about initiation can help eliminate some of these patterns. Here are some guiding questions:

- Who tends to initiate sex more often?
- To the partner who initiates more, how do you feel about this? To the partner who doesn't, how do you feel about initiating?
- Have either one of you pulled back from initiating? Why?
- What would help you (both) feel safe initiating sex?
- How do you agree to handle a no if one of you initiates but the other doesn't want to?

Quick tip: Sometimes scheduling sex can help in this area. Another tool is to use visual cues. When both partners feel nervous about initiating, it can be helpful to decide on a cue that lets your partner know that you're in the mood. This is a more passive approach to rebuilding comfortability when initiating, but it gets the job done.

bring it home

Our homes serve as one of the most important instruments of change when it comes to making massive societal movement. Granted, these moves will take time, but if you look back even one generation, I guarantee that there are tangible and palpable shifts in how that generation functioned differently than yours. I want you to find hope in this sentiment. So often when it comes to the mental load, women can get stuck on the need for massive societal change in order for things to be any different. What would happen if women were paid a fair wage, childcare became more affordable, men had more time off, or women actually had support around childbirth? The list goes on and on and these things are big. They're game changers. They would make a considerable difference in the experience of mothers and our home and family life.

However, it's not the *only* mechanism of change. When we ascribe to the belief that meaningful change can only occur when systemic changes happen, then we're sort of rendered helpless. What's the average woman to do? Likely she's already managing the mental load, working in some capacity, or nurturing a side hustle, while juggling the kids and trying to eke in morsels of personal care to preserve some of her sanity and sense of self, and now she's supposed to phone her senator?

I mean, if you've got it in you, go! But for the majority of us, this isn't necessarily something we're devoting our lives to changing. Still, we feel the pains of the lack of change, so what the heck are we supposed to do? My advice is that we work to change our homes, and here's why.

You can work to change society from a top-down approach or a bottom-up. Both matter and both make an impact. The top-down approach requires making changes at the federal and state level. It requires political backing and probably capital. It requires companies to get on board and see the critical need to care for employees and their home and family life differently. To see past just the bottom line. I'm hopeful that we will get here, but this isn't the only way to make change. Change can also happen from the bottom up. I believe the place that we have the most agency is at home. We're already working hard as parents and partners, but let's be mindful about how this can be a powerful place to institute change around the mental load. It actually doesn't require much, if any, extra work. Ideally, both the bottom-up and top-down approaches are happening simultaneously, but I don't want anyone to use the excuse of "Nothing can get better until society as a whole is different" as a reason not to take action at home around the mental load. If you really analyze this stance, it's helpless—without a sense of control or personal power—and it's inaccurate. A lot can be done to make changes when you start at home.

Our change at home can change the world. What our children experience, are taught, and observe in our home will shape the people they will become, the expectations they will have for their partners, and the partners they will become. When we do things differently at home, it creates a ripple effect that continues to grow and impact future generations. The millennial generation and Gen Z are known for being cycle breakers and working to raise emotionally intelligent kids. Why? Because we hope that this will improve their lives and that they will have healthier relationships. We work to change our parenting to change their future. The same idea applies when we teach kids to be thoughtful of the home and family life: The way they will operate in their future families will shift. We may not do it perfectly, but our contribution will matter in immeasurable ways.

In this chapter, I'm going to give you some key areas to consider in your home to help your children be more aware of and participate in the mental load. I will also offer a practical tool for doing this. Please note, this entire book has been devoted to helping you and your partner relate differently to each other and the mental load, so know that if you've made changes in that department, you're already doing a ton of good for your children. They absorb so much of what they witness, and seeing how you and your partner care for each other, communicate openly and graciously, and work well together is already impacting them in important ways.

When You're the Only One Vacuuming the Garage

"Mom, no one actually vacuums their garage," I'd exclaim upon seeing my mom lugging the thousand-pound Kirby toward the door leading to our Ohio garage. My mom would respond with an edge in her voice, now aggressively vacuuming, with something like "I'll take care of it—don't even worry about it." It's wild how being a grown-up gives you a completely new perspective on things your own parents have done, said, stressed about, or asked you to do. What a jerk I was for not just grabbing the Kirby and taking care of the garage floor for her. My parents didn't really ask much of my sister and me in terms of chores or responsibilities around the house. We both were pretty busy with sports, and when a freak illness cut my running career short, I started working before my sixteenth birthday. I think this is in part why they went easy on us at home—but the work still needed to be done, and because my mom was a stay-at-home mom who took a lot of joy in caring for our family, it fell on her. Now, I know my dad will read this and say, "Hey! I was involved." Of course he was, but the majority of the management of the home fell on my mom (still does), and I don't think she was bothered by this.

You can love caring for your home and family and also get irritated when you feel like you're carrying it all, and this is something I know my mom felt from time to time. The garage incident was one of those moments. She'd be tense, huffy, and make statements under her breath about doing it herself. I think we all know this place. And being in this state is discouraging on several levels. One, you feel angry and frustrated because you are carrying it mostly alone, and ultimately you start having pangs of resentment toward your family. Two, you likely hate that it brings out the worst in you, causing you to act like a grump when you know you're not. This doesn't feel fair either. I know that when my mom was in one of these places, I wanted to stay as far away as possible. It's so incredibly unfair looking back because she needed my help, not my retreat. She needed me to offer appreciation or take initiative, not avoid her and what needed to be done. This isn't any different from many of the couple dynamics that end up playing out in relationships.

One of the goals of shifting the mental load at home is creating an atmosphere of teamwork and sharing the responsibilities for helping the family and home to function. Maybe you'll still feel, overall, like the manager with your kids, but if you could move the needle to feel this way less often, what a difference it would make in your relationship with them and your overall experience in your home life. Oh, and I have to confess, now that I have my own home, I've vacuumed the garage more times than I can count, and every time, I think of my mom and I laugh at the irony.

I want to share three goals when it comes to involving your kids more around the home.

Goal 1: Instilling a Family Team Mentality

If you have kids that are of talking age, it's not long until you hear some version of the phrase "I didn't make that mess" or "I didn't get that out" from one of your kids when you ask them to take care of something. The idea that we're only responsible for what is ours seems like it's almost the default response. I'm not sure where we pick this up. Regardless, it's crazy-making when you're the parent who's doing everything for everyone else and then your kid responds with this attitude. "Seriously, just pick up the dang Legos." Or if you're really at your wit's end, you'll remind your kids that at least they don't have to farm for their food and it wasn't that long ago that kids worked in factories. Likely not your best parenting moment but relatable and understandable for sure.

Here's the thing: Our homes need to be collectivist ecosystems where we all have each other's backs and take care of our home because it's a shared space that we all benefit from. A simple strategy for increasing a family team mentality is involving your kids more in the regular stuff you do around the home. The younger the better (because younger kids are more eager), but it's never too late. This invitation works because it isn't a demand, which naturally stirs up a desire to resist; it teaches kids life skills and what needs done around the home; and it incorporates togetherness, which is an excellent motivator. It's also a powerful yet simple technique for most kids who desire to have more responsibility and trust given to them. I know our son feels a sense of accomplishment when he lugs heavy grocery bags up the stairs (also good for regulation) and our daughter loves the independence when she brings in the garbage cans by herself.

The way that we serve up these "chores" to our kids can make all the difference. If they seem like a drag, it will feel that way. Any opportunity to gamify work around the house, set a timer to it, or add some music will also help to shift the mood. Our son finds music really regulating, so whenever he has some tasks he needs to do, he cranks up his music and dances while he does it.

Another way to foster a team mentality is through the language you use. See the table below for examples.

Instead of	Try
"Hey, will you *help me* do . . ." (this implies you own it versus something that just needs to be done)	"The groceries are here; let's carry them up together."
"Can't you just do what I asked?"	"I know you didn't leave that out, but we're a family team and we all work together to keep our home put together."
"Fine, I'll just pick this stuff up."	"If you don't pick up these things, who do you think does? We're a family team and right now I'm doing XYZ to help our family."

Goal 2: Increasing Initiative Taking

Initiative taking is one of the most requested changes women have for their partners around the mental load. Imagine if parents actively worked to increase this skill set in their kids so that when they entered adult relationships, it was something they already did naturally. Cue angels singing from above. It would be heavenly, right?

I think this is one of the most important skills to teach our kids when it comes to the mental load because it will impact the quality of your home life, who your kid will become as a future partner, and will help to cut back on the burnout and resentment so many mothers feel. The benefit of initiative taking is that you get to step out of the roles of task manager and nag and get to ditch the running to-do list you're carrying around, not only what you have to take care of, but also what your kids need to take care of. Ultimately, we want to raise humans who can function on their own as responsible adults; part of this is teaching them how to take initiative and complete tasks without us managing them. They have to learn to be self-managers.

I recognize that this will be a skill set that will develop over time, and depending on the age of your kids, you may be able to do a little in this department or a lot in this department, so adjust accordingly. Later I will share a major tool I use to help develop this skill set, but know that some key phrases can be very helpful when it comes to increasing initiative taking.

When you think of how to develop this skill, know that the formula for initiative taking is

Observation + Action = Initiative

When you keep this formula in mind, you can use it to guide how you handle different situations and respond to your kids. Ultimately, you want to work to increase their observational skills and how often they take action based on their observations.

Here are some key phrases I use on repeat:

Goal	Example	Rationale
To get the kids to do something that they didn't do but should have	"Oh, hey, your pajamas are on the floor in the bathroom."	All I do is make an observation. I do *not* give a command unless they don't do anything, but nine times out of ten the observation prompts action. The win is that they aren't feeling like I'm bossing or nagging them and I am helping them increase both observational skills and action skills and making them aware of an expectation that pajamas (or whatever) don't go on the bathroom floor.
To get the kids to tidy up a part of the house	"Please go to the living room and see what needs to be done and take care of it." Alternative: "Please go into the living room and notice three things that need to be done and take care of them."	This is a prompt for the kids to practice observing and acting without being given any specific direction. If the kids like to feel powerful and don't like to feel bossed around, this really works well because they get to choose what they do. Also, it spares you from making a list and spelling it all out. Less work on you; building skill sets for them.
To help the kids increase their observational skills	"When you took care of the living room, what didn't you do that still needs to be done?"	This helps the kids recognize what it would take to "finish" the job and also observe what they didn't do that still needs to be done, which increases awareness around the home.
To help kids increase ownership	"When I explain it again, it uses a lot of my energy. You tell me how you think it needs to be done and I'll let you know if there are any changes."	This helps kids take more ownership over a task or job and spares the parent of being the owner, regulator, and enforcer of "correct."
To help kids look for their own stuff before asking you	"Where have you looked already?"	This allows you to not have to be the one who keeps track of where everything is and helps your kids take responsibility for their belongings.
To help kids learn the steps on their own	"What's the next step in what you need to do?"	Our kids are quick to come to us for answers, but by helping them learn to solve issues on their own, they will know how to do it the next time around.

Goal 3: Influencing Who They Will Be as a Future Partner

The final goal is that you want to consider how you are shaping who they will be as a future partner. This isn't often the lens we use when parenting. We think about raising a good human or citizen but not really a future partner. I know plenty of people who are good humans or neighbors but drop the ball on being a good partner. If you can remember way back to the chapters on expectations, I talked about how we develop templates that click into place for different roles we have in our life. The role of partner has its own template; there's more wrapped up into this title than just neighbor or friend. And just like you have been influenced by what you saw and experienced in your own home, your children will be too. Therefore, think about how you want to cultivate a spirit of mutual caretaking, generosity, graciousness, and non-defensiveness in your own home with your kids. Also think about what they see between you and your partner and how this will shape who they are as a partner and what they will look for in a future partner.

If you have a daughter, what she sees in her mom as a woman and a wife will impact what she expects of herself. What she sees from your husband will shape how she thinks about men and the treatment she thinks is normal. It will shape her expectations.

If you have a son, what he sees in his father will shape what he expects of himself. What he sees modeled by his mother will shape what he expects out of his female relationships and what treatment he thinks is normal and acceptable.

When you think of parenting in this way—I'm raising future partners and shaping their relationship standards—it really changes everything. This alone could be an entire book (and maybe it will be someday), but I hope that this lens helps you and your partner align on some very important areas of raising kids. If you need a baseline place to start, ask your kids, "What do you think it means to be married?" or "What do you notice about Mom and Dad's marriage?" If you're ready to jump into exploring this concept with your partner, here are some questions to help guide this conversation:

1. When our kids think back to our marriage, what do we want to really stand out? How can we cultivate more of this?
2. What kind of partner do we want our kids to commit to? Are we being those partners in our own relationship?
3. How do we want to actively teach our kids to be good future partners? What qualities do we want to instill in them? What skills do we want to help them to develop?

Get in the Zone

I sat across the table from my friend at Whole Foods. She has kids the same age as my kids and they've been the sweetest of friends since they were babies. We live about an hour apart and so we were finding random places to hang that day to extend our time together, hence the Whole Foods hangout. My friend is Danish and grew up in Denmark and met her husband, an American, in her early twenties. She loves her native culture and I am blessed to be the recipient of her stories, which enrich my life in many ways. Over her pizza and my beef and broccoli, we discussed differences in expectations of kids in Denmark versus the US. For example, she was responsible for cooking dinner once a week when she was young, and she now puts this into practice with her kids (ages ten and eight at the time of this conversation). She shared with me an ingenious tip for helping the kids take more responsibility around the home that I'm so grateful to pass on to you. Before I share, know this: You can start this at a very young age (approximately four years old), but you know your kids best, so make adjustments as necessary. No pressure here. Also, you don't need to be super rigid about it. There aren't rules or right or wrong ways of implementing this; it's a loose framework that helps to achieve the three goals previously discussed.

The tip is to give kids a zone of the house that they are responsible for managing. Here are the requirements:

1. The zone has to be a shared space.
2. The zone has to be a space that is manageable based on your kid's age. For example, our daughter, Effie, is responsible

for the living room. She has to fold blankets, fix the throw pillows, toss any random snack wrappers that are thrown around the couch, etc.

Here's why this approach is so genius:

- It teaches observational skills because your child is regularly having to check their zone and see what is out of place.
- It teaches initiative taking because once they observe what's needed to be done, they're responsible for handling it.
- It requires very little nagging and absolutely no list making, which saves your headspace and doesn't make you feel like a grump. If they need to be reminded (and they will), just ask, "Have you checked your zone?" Done.
- It gives them ownership, and most kids feel a sense of pride in taking care of a space. Nine times out of ten when our kids finish up their zone, they want us to see all that they did. This helps cut down on the pushback so often associated with doling out a chore and instead cultivates a sense of ownership.
- It cultivates a teamwork mentality because you're putting them in charge of a shared space. This means that they may be picking up their sister's Legos or carrying in a water glass you left on an end table. It challenges the idea that we're only responsible for our own spaces and belongings and helps kids to be involved in the overall caretaking of the home.

Remember, this doesn't need to be rigid. You will have to remind them, and you can make any tweaks and adjustments you want along the way, like switching zones after a while. However, this approach is an incredibly simple yet powerful way to involve your kids more in caring for your home.

A Note on Chore Charts

I don't actually mind task lists (we use ClickCharts to help our kids remember what needs to be done on school days to get out of the house) because they can help your kids stay on task, know what needs to be done, and take care of things on their own without you having to guide the process too much.

However, there is another perspective on chore charts and lists that is worth sharing: They may perpetuate the idea that you are the one that is responsible for delegating all the things that need to be done. It may continue to feed the notion that you own it all until others are told what to do. I don't want to add more stress to your life—if these charts and lists work for you, you do you, my friend. But this is a perspective worth considering. Plus, in my experience, these chore charts and lists require full-on nag mode: "Did you do your chores?" and "No video games until your chores are done!" and so on. So now you're making the list and enforcing it too. It may be easier to use the zone approach and then add more zones as your kids get older and can take on more. Again, do what works best for your family.

Take It Easy

I want to offer you a reminder to go easy on yourself through all of this. In the realm of parenting, we tend to really outdo ourselves, and then burn ourselves out big time. You don't need to know the perfect phrases; I am just offering ideas to help you use your brain a little less. Your five-year-old doesn't need to already be making dinners; don't stress yourself out over teaching your kids all the things all at once. In the time of intensive parenting, the last thing I want to do is stress you out or add more to your plate. Remember that you're already parenting. You're already teaching these things. I'm just offering some organization, intention, and framework to what you're already doing. My suggestion would be to choose one thing to cultivate and then sprinkle it into your life. Don't do an overhaul, just a little shift. Each little shift will add up to make a major difference.

conclusion

Throughout the writing of this book, I've struggled with deep insecurity around it being *helpful enough*. More than ever, I want this book to enrich your life and relationships, and my hope is that you gleaned practical tools and insights and, ideally, that you have made some major shifts around the mental load. However, I recognize that relationship shifts are almost always slow and take repetition. I think my insecurity around this being *helpful enough* is just another side of wanting changes in relationships to be quick and easy. It's the desire I have to offer you a magic-wand solution, when I know that's not realistic or sustainable. It's the awareness I have that making changes can be a grind and may require sitting in the yuck of uncomfortable conversations more than once. It can feel hard and painful. I wanted to spare you all of that, yet I know that's not possible or really going to help. I hope this book offers guidance as you've navigated these changes, and I want to commend you for being courageous as you've stepped into making meaningful changes in your relationship. It's worth it.

Before we end our time together, I wanted to offer you some reminders.

1. **You can't overdose on appreciation.** Appreciation always feels good. Some people will feel a little uncomfortable receiving it, and tons of people will feel uncomfortable slathering it on, but it's an easy way to show love to those you care about. Offer appreciation as much as you can, even for the little things. When you express appreciation to one another, you don't feel

taken for granted, which is a major source of disconnection, resentment, and growing apart.

2. **Being generous is (almost) always a good choice.** Being generous goes along with appreciation. But you can be generous in other ways, like how you shape your story about your partner. You can be generous in how you show affection, praise your partner, touch them throughout the day, give to them freely, and in how you meet their needs. I recognize that this can become unhealthy when it's severely lopsided, so please keep tabs on this, but know that experimenting with some extra generosity is a good way to soften the tone and increase warmth in your relationship.

3. **Reassurance is a powerful tool.** If both partners want to feel loved and secure in their relationship, then reassurance becomes a simple tool to bolster these feelings. When you reassure your partner, "I can hear your needs," or "You are a good partner, even when I ask for a need," or "I'm not going to leave you just because I'm hurt right now," or "I love you when you're stressed and when you're calm," it strengthens feelings of safety and love. Reassurance builds connection and bridges to one another that allow you both to more easily cross to the other's perspective and side.

4. **Expect setbacks with change.** Real change rarely happens overnight, so please be patient with yourself and your partner. Notice the good, comment on the work they're putting in, and continue to move forward trying new skills and approaches. I mentioned earlier in the book that relationship changes may feel mechanical at first and then later they will become automatic—please remember this. It's okay to feel awkward; remember the outcome you're after and use that as your motivation to continue on. Expect that there will be backslides when change occurs. New things will not permanently stick the first time, so get in the practice of course correcting often in your relationship. When you actually do your mental load meeting, you will have a scheduled mechanism to help implement these course corrections. So really do them—they will help you.

5. **Small improvements add up to major changes.** Continuing

with the last point, remember that small improvements in your relationship will add up to major changes, so continue to reinforce the effort along the way. Offer yourself praise when you do something differently that supports your relationship.

6. **Be a pipe cleaner, not a spaghetti noodle.** This comes from an illustration I used to talk to our kids about flexibility, so I'll offer it to you. Some people approach things like raw spaghetti noodles: inflexible, unwavering, and seeking perfection. What happens when you try to bend raw spaghetti? It breaks. Much like how perfectionists end up running themselves ragged or stubborn partners end up broken and alone in their own stubbornness. Others are like cooked spaghetti: incredibly accommodating, bendy, and you can literally abuse it and it will stick to a wall. Over time, cooked spaghetti starts to lose its shape from contorting to accommodate everyone and everything.

I want to encourage you to be a pipe cleaner in your relationship. Be flexible and consider ways you may be too rigid and need to bend a bit more. When you're a pipe cleaner you have bendability but you maintain your shape. You have a backbone, you stick up for yourself, but you are able to flex and curve in order to care for your relationship and home. Resolving the mental load often requires a little conflict and lots of compromise and cooperation.

Thank you for reading this book and for working to shift the mental load in your home and family. The differences you're making in your home matter. Your relationship will feel lighter and more joyful. Your relationship with your kids (if you have them) will shift because when you feel appreciated and that things are fair, you won't harbor resentment or suffer from as much overwhelm, making you better able to enjoy your kids and be the version of yourself you always hoped to be. Your changes will also help to change what the mental load and family life looks like for future generations. Your effort, time, and work matters. Thank you.

If you enjoyed this book, please share it with a person you know and love.

appendix

Let's Troubleshoot

I'm hoping that this section offers some targeted support around the mental load and hang-ups you may encounter with your partner.

Some of these scripts may seem condescending. I want you to know a couple of things. First, tone matters, so the feeling of the script can change based on how you speak it. Second, some of these scripts are confrontational, and you will sense that from the words. The reality is, in relationships, sometimes you have to battle a bit for your perspective to be acknowledged and heard. People often will speak without really thinking through what they're saying or the deeper implications of their language and words. My goal here is to offer you scripts that help you confront the statements made by your partner in a way that requires them to actually reflect on what they're saying and explain it to you. In many ways, it's breaking down their logic so you can discuss the issue in a way that leads to a solution that works for you both and for them to take responsibility for their approach and how it's negatively impacting you and your relationship.

I voice a need and he doesn't respond. It makes me feel invisible.

This is so frustrating; I'm so sorry. This is a perfect moment to shift from the content of the conversation to the process. Here are some examples of what you could say:

> "I'm noticing that you're starting to check out of this conversation. What happened just now?"

"I'm noticing that you are shutting down. Would you be up for pausing and coming back later to pick back up? How much time do you need? This is important to me, so I really want to make sure we talk about this."

Here are some alternative scripts for discussing this outside of the present moment:

"I've noticed that whenever I bring up XYZ, you tend to shut down or get really quiet. Can you tell me what's going on for you in those moments?"

"When you shut down during our conversations, I feel stuck and hopeless about how we can work on XYZ. What would help you to feel better talking about this with me?"

"It seems like when I bring up wanting to talk to you about something in our relationship, you immediately shut down or disengage. How can I approach you differently so you can have this conversation with me?"

"I have to be able to communicate with you without you feeling like everything I say is a criticism. I love you and am after connection not criticism. Can we come up with some solutions to navigate these talks better?"

My husband has ADHD (he's on medication) but he's constantly forgetting things all the time. I'm sick of reminding him and feeling like a nag.

When you have a partner with ADHD, it can make navigating the mental load a little trickier. There is a real justification if your partner is having trouble remembering things and keeping him or herself organized. Specifically, people with ADHD often struggle with navigating the mental load, because it requires a combination of skills that are directly impacted by ADHD symptoms, such as planning, prioritizing, time management, and working memory. The mental load involves keeping track of invisible tasks—anticipating needs, remembering deadlines, and coordinating responsibilities, all of which can feel overwhelming when executive functioning challenges come into play. For example, someone with ADHD may forget key details, have difficulty initiating tasks, or feel paralyzed by decision fatigue. Additionally, the emotional toll of consistently falling behind or feeling like they're letting their partner down can lead to frustration or avoidance, further compounding the issue. With ADHA the mental load isn't just a list of tasks; it's a mountain of cognitive demands that can be incredibly hard to scale without effective strategies and systems in place.

There are three components that are really important to navigating the mental load when you or your partner has ADHD:

1. Systems
2. Structure
3. Personal accountability

When you talk about how to navigate the mental load differently, discuss some specific systems you would like to implement in your home. Some of these may be really simple, like "Keys always go in this basket on the counter," or more involved, like having a digital calendar to help organize lists, schedules, and tasks. Your partner can have their own daily planning ritual to create lists, schedule activities, or check or input information. Here are some examples:

- Use your weekly SHARE Agenda (or increase the frequency) to prioritize tasks.
- Use visual organization tools like a digital calendar, family whiteboard, or color-coded calendar, which can be helpful for partners with ADHD.
- Use task management apps to help you organize tasks together. You can usually set reminders in these, so make sure you really make them work for you. Keep in mind it may be difficult for someone with ADHD to determine how urgent a task is. As you discuss what you're sharing, also talk about what level of priority the task is (i.e., "urgent" to "on your own time").

- Use external methods like alarms, alerts, reminders, or timers to stay on task.

Ultimately the partner with ADHD has to take personal accountability for creating and sticking with the systems. Sure, you can collaborate together to come up with what works, but do not make your partner the one in charge of managing *your* systems.

He constantly assumes I have a mental load because I just think too much about it. Or he sees it as something I'm choosing and tells me, "Just don't concern yourself with it then."

There are so many variables to these situations, because sometimes we do take on things that are unnecessary or we have standards that are so intense that we burn ourselves to the ground. Self-assess on this one and ask yourself if there are some things you can let go. Is there any truth to this? My first book, *Love Your Kids Without Losing Yourself*, is a good read for working through some self-reflection and adjustment pieces.

With that being said, let's assume your standards are reasonable. When this conversation has been had over and over, it means that you may have to up the level of confrontation. Here are some sample scripts:

"When you respond this way, it leaves me feeling really alone in my overwhelm because your answer is essentially, 'This is your problem; you deal with it.' Is this how you're wanting me to feel?"

"Okay, so what do you think I'm choosing to do that is just optional for our family life? And if I stop doing these things, who does them? That's the piece that continues to really confuse me when you respond this way. It's like you make it my problem, just tell me to drop it, but then you don't participate in picking it up or troubleshooting. Ultimately I feel unappreciated and undervalued when you talk to me this way."

He says that since he works and I'm a SAHM, my job is the home and family.

This pushback is tricky, because it often conjures up a deep feeling of insecurity and guilt about your right to ask for more participation in the home and family life. When a partner responds in this way, it can be hard to know how to respond and way too easy to just shut down and end the conversation. I want to remind you of something and offer you one alternative perspective.

1. Remember the currency of home and family life is time and energy, not necessarily money.
2. Try framing your time at home as a job too. Even though it's unpaid, there's no denying it's work. Consider this: When you're both at work, you each do your part. One makes the money and one takes care of the home and family. Now, when you both are home together, it doesn't make sense for one of you to continue working into oblivion and the other to be "off." Instead view time at home as the shared time of the day when you both can negotiate who does what based on who has time and energy.

This conversation can easily get confrontational. Here are some sample scripts if you continue to get pushback.

"So I hear you saying that when you're home, you're off work and it's my job to do all things home and family. But when do I get to be 'off' or get any sort of reprieve?"

"This is not a threat, but you should know that when I ask you to participate more at home and you argue with me, I end up feeling unimportant, and it's eventually going to cause resentment in our relationship. It's not good for us to be in this place."

I'm already feeling resentment. Now what?

This could be an entire book in itself, but I want you to revisit chapter 10. Recovering from resentment is a joint responsibility in that your partner will have to incorporate changes and you will have to rebuild your trust and positive attitude toward them. Therefore, when you're healing from resentment, you will have to intentionally work to shift how you see your partner. If you've been steeping in resentment, you have likely been focusing on the worst in your partner, so take ownership: Shift where you place your focus and highlight qualities about your partner that make your life better.

Additionally, healing from resentment requires that the "offense" that has led to it stops and a new and more positive behavior takes its place. If your partner is not incorporating more positive behaviors, it will be difficult to move out of resentment. Therefore, this becomes an area of negotiation, discussion, and possible confrontation. Many of the scripts offered throughout this section will be helpful.

He gets so triggered by the mention of any inequity, so the conversation is impossible.

You can review the section on the deficit default response in chapter 4, but here are some scripts that can help you know how to respond. Another approach is to label it differently; if "inequity" is triggering, call it something else.

"We have to be able to talk about this. What is so threatening about the mention of inequity?"

"I notice you get so bugged by the mention of inequity, so you can call it what you want. I don't want to argue about who does more; it doesn't matter because we're in this together. The piece that really matters is that I feel [insert feeling: e.g., invisible, unappreciated, unfairness] and it's impacting our relationship. When you shut down the ability to talk about this, it just means that I either stuff what I feel and get resentful or get loud, creating more issues between us. We need to figure out a way of talking about this without it spiraling out of control. How can I bring this up to you in a way that you can handle talking about it?"

My husband likes to tell me to just hire it out.

This one is tricky because this is a generous offer but also comes with some caveats. You have to decide here if this works for you and your family and who actually manages the hiring it out, because that is an entire job in itself. Here are some follow-up points worth discussing with your partner:

> "Okay, I'm happy to get this hired out. But who finds the person and then manages the person we hire? Is that on me?"
>
> "Oh, I like that idea. Will you take on finding someone and scheduling this?"
>
> "When you tell me to hire someone, I still have to research who to hire and then manage that person. I appreciate the offer, but sometimes it just feels like you're dismissing the job like you don't have time for it and putting it back on me to manage outsourcing it. It would be more helpful if . . ."

**My partner travels or works shift work,
so I can't even hand things off.**

I live this life too; it can be really challenging. You have to get really comfortable asking for what you need. If you're carrying the weight of the home front, it's easy to click into a gear where you just do it all. Additionally, it can be really difficult to transition to having your partner home. Here are some tips:

- Make sure you do your SHARE meeting. I cannot stress enough how this will help you stay connected and help your partner, who is out of the house often, feel more in the know with family life.
- Sometimes what you can't get in deeds, you will need to get in words. This requires that you work to get good at expressing appreciation of each other. When your partner can't be there in person, they need to encourage you with their words. It makes a huge difference.

- Create a homecoming ritual. This looks different for every family, but what are some staples you want to include? Maybe it's a really positive greeting when they get home, a date night, a tapping in and tapping out, a reset period and then trading off. You decide together, but this makes a huge difference.
- Use digital calendars or apps to stay in the know with schedules. This helps the absent partner to be more aware and also gives them the ability to jump back in when they return home.

I get to a breaking point and then just snap. Not good.

This falls under taking personal accountability for how you show up in your relationship. If this happens, it likely means that you bottle things up and then you blow up. To change this requires that you get better at hitting the release valve more often. If you and your partner have your SHARE meeting, it will dramatically minimize how much this happens because you'll have a forum for talking about what's going on in your relationship. Things won't have the opportunity to build. Also, paying attention to how you craft your story about your partner may help you regularly clean out your attitude toward them, which can also prevent snapping as often.

He won't take on mental load because of not enough sex.
I don't want sex because I feel like I don't have a partner.

You can read about this in chapter 20 under the sexual standoff section. This is a really common dynamic where partners decide to not give until they get. You may not love this answer, but someone has to make the step toward the other. There has to be one partner who decides, *You know what, I'm stepping out of this power struggle*. It can also be helpful to call out the dynamic. It can sound like this:

> "Hey, I'm noticing we're stuck in a struggle where we both want something from each other but are unwilling to budge until we get what we want. I wonder if we can come up with a compromise to help us break out of this place."

He says I'm making a bigger deal about the mental load because it's trendy on social media.

This one feels like a total cop-out. I don't deny that when you see something on social media over and over again it can start to fire you up. There's real truth to that, so you have to take some responsibility for what you consume and how much of it you consume. However, it doesn't make the experience and what you feel fake or made up. Social media defined an experience shared by millions of women; part of why it's "trendy" is because it's so relatable and women who have struggled with the feeling now don't feel so alone.

The logic here is flawed. It's akin to saying, "The cancer won't kill you if the doctor doesn't diagnose it." You'd say that's ridiculous, and in this case the logic isn't any different. Maybe before seeing it on social media you felt the impact of the mental load; social media just diagnosed what you were feeling. Regardless, the impact of the mental load (diagnosed or not) can eat away at your relationship health. Explore this logic with your partner.

Secondly, what's their point? Is the point to say you don't actually feel that way? This is invalidating and completely ignoring a real experience. Here are some responses:

> "What's your point? And what do you want me to feel when you say this? I'm not sure I'm understanding your argument or how this gets us to a better place."
>
> "The point is, whether it's on social media or not, I've felt this way for a long time. I just have a term for it now. If it impacts our relationship, wouldn't you be invested in working on this with me?"

He wants me to make lists.

Review the chapter on taking ownership and collecting data. Lists are a trigger for a lot of women because it keeps them in the position of still being the owner of all the information and tasks and it suggests that their partner has no responsibility in actually thinking through these things. Here are some potential responses:

"You make the list and I'll check it."

"When you ask me to make the list, it implies that I own it and then I have to manage you. You put a list together, and I will, too, and then we will compare notes."

"I want to get to a place where me making the list is the exception and not the rule because it means that I never actually get relieved from thinking all this stuff through and carrying it in my brain. It makes me your boss when we both are responsible for our family and home."

He will help, but then it goes back to normal.

When anyone is implementing new changes, it's normal for setbacks to occur; however, when nothing actually sticks, it can be really frustrating. Here are some scripts for confronting the lack of change and follow-through:

"I am feeling frustrated because I've expressed to you that I really would love to see some changes in this area but nothing seems to be changing. I want you to know that I won't be doing XYZ anymore."

"We've had this conversation more times than I care to admit, but it seems like nothing changes. Can we talk about what's getting in the way of this shift?"

"I want you to know this change is really important to me. Is there something I can clarify to help make it happen?"

We both work full-time, but I make a fraction of what he does, so he thinks this means he's off the hook.

Review chapter 3 on the lie, and have your partner read that section. Work to have a conversation around the currency of your home being time and energy instead of money. Additional confrontation points are "Don't you want to be involved in the family and home?" and "What kind of partner/parent did you imagine you'd be?"

Hardship Olympics. He's more tired than me.

I covered this pattern when I discussed the deficit default. But here's another script and some information to take into consideration.

Often this type of response signals parallel needs, which means that both partners have unmet needs. The one partner just picks a terrible time to bring theirs up.

- You can respond with empathy and then move back into what you're asking for.
- You can call out the potential missing need: "I just expressed a need and you responded with your own need instead of acknowledging mine. Is there something you need in this moment?"
- Or get more confrontational:

Partner 1: *Expresses a need.*

Partner 2: *"You're tired? Well, I'm tired too. I just worked all day."*

Partner 1: *"When you respond that way, it's really an unfair way to argue, because you just breeze by what I said and now we are competing to prove who is more tired. We can both be tired. However, we can address what I do another time if it bothers you. But right now I want to just keep this conversation about what I'm bringing up."*

Partner 2: *"So I can't express what I feel?"*

Partner 1: *"You can express what you feel but your timing is suspicious. If you feel this way, why do you wait until I bring it up first? It's hard for me not to think that it's a way to derail our conversation or confuse things. It feels like tit for tat and that's not fair. If you want to discuss it and it's important to you, let's set up a separate time to talk."*

My desire is that these scripts and strategies help you navigate the stickier spots with your partner. I know how hard it can be to enter into conflict or push through the uncomfortable conversations. You're courageous for trying and I hope your relationship will be better for it.

additional resources

- **Expectations Worksheet:** A printable based on the exercises from chapter 11 to help you unearth your hidden expectations.

- **How You Show Up Exercise:** Sometimes we don't even realize the relationship-wrecking behaviors that we engage in. This printable exercise from page 172 will help you reflect on how you're showing up in your relationship and how you can make meaningful changes.

- **Mental Load List:** This resource provides five common aspects of the mental load and breaks down the mental, physical, and emotional pieces involved in fully completing them. Download this spreadsheet to divvy up or delegate tasks with your partner or decide to drop them.

- **SHARE Agenda:** A printable version of the SHARE meeting from pages 213–215 to help you and your partner stay on track.

- **Sex Ed 101 Books:** A link to my most recommended books on caring for your sexual relationship.

acknowledgments

This is always one of the hardest parts of my book to write, because the immense amount of gratitude and appreciation I feel toward those who have been part of my book journey is incredibly hard to capture in words. Here goes nothing.

Thank you to my husband, Chad, and our kids, Effie and Roy. My husband travels regularly for work, so I am the stable force at home. Whenever I have more going on in my life, it shakes up everyone's lives. The kids see me a little less; Chad has to jump in after being gone and take over the home front. It's a united effort. You all have been such amazing supporters of me. No one complained; instead, you all just cheered me on. You are my most favorite people in the world, my encouragers, and you make my life so much richer. Thank you for your sacrifice and for all the love you show me.

Thank you to my parents. You have provided me with an incredible example of what a happy and healthy relationship looks like. You love each other so well. Mom, thank you for your pep talks and encouraging me when self-doubt crept in. Dad, thank you for all of your mentorship. You have one of the most beautiful minds of anyone I know, and I'm grateful to have learned so much from you. In a previous life—when kids weren't in the picture and I wasn't seemingly always on a time restriction—our meandering, lengthy conversations happened far more frequently. Now with kids and obligations, these conversations are some of my most treasured times with you.

Thank you to my sister, Jess. I see you and all that you do to carry the load in your home and family life. You're an incredible mother to some of the most adorable kids, and I love you so much.

Thank you to my in-laws, Cindy and Larry. I will never be able to say this enough. Thank you for raising a son who is so devoted to his family and for letting me be the leading lady in his life. I love you both.

Thank you to my editor, Brigitta Nortker. I handed you a stream of consciousness on just about all the things I've wanted to say about this topic for five-plus years, and you made sense of it all and gave it a digestible organization. I am incredibly grateful you exist, because doing what you do just makes me want to take a nap. Thank you for cheering this book on, advocating for me, pouring your thoughtfulness into it, and sending me all your rom-com book suggestions.

Thank you to my friend Kelly, for always being such a willing reader and offering me the most thoughtful feedback. I'm not sure if I'll ever be able to fully express how much your friendship means to me. Female friendships are tricky, and yours has offered a reparative experience for me. I feel such a kinship with you and am forever grateful that our paths crossed.

Thank you to my friend Myla. Turns out it's entirely possible to build and nurture a friendship almost exclusively through voice notes. Ha! I adore you, appreciate your endless ideas and feedback, and am so grateful for you. Thank you for your friendship.

To Alex and Lindsey, my very first friends in California, who have both moved way too far away. Even though distance separates us, I always know you're there for me and cheering me on. Alex, you have such an incredible mind and are always willing to peel apart any issue until the core is reached. You get me and have always seen my heart. Thank you for your friendship. Lindsey, thank you for always treating my dreams like "Duh, of course you can do that." You pushed me to jump out of my comfort zone and start an Instagram account, and it changed my life. Thank you.

Thank you to my new friend Sarah. I have loved getting to know you, and I feel indebted for the way you have championed my work to numerous Mom Co. groups and invited me to speak at Mom Con. It was an absolute honor to share with so many incredible moms, and I know I was there because of you. Thank you, big time!

To my agent, Rachel Jacobson, and the entire Thomas Nelson team (Kathryn Duke, Kristen Golden, Claire Drake, and Lisa Beech) who have helped bring this book to life. I am beyond grateful to have so many strong and thoughtful women supporting this book and helping me along the way. I have absolutely adored working with you all.

Thank you to the men and women who participated in the survey and interviews I conducted early in this book-writing process. I am honored that you took time out of your lives to share your stories with me.

Thank you to my Instagram community. I am regularly humbled that I have the privilege of being able to share my thoughts and suggestions with you. What an honor it is to play any part, no matter how small, in your life. I hope that what I share with you has been helpful. Thank you for your support and your trust.

notes

Chapter 2: it's not you; it's the mental load

1. Emma Clit, "You Should've Asked," Emma, May 20, 2017, https:// english.emmaclit.com/2017/05/20/you-shouldve-asked/.
2. Melissa Hogenboom, "The Hidden Load: How 'Thinking of Everything' Holds Mums Back," BBC, May 18, 2021, https://www .bbc.com/worklife/article/20210518-the-hidden-load-how-thinking -of-everything-holds-mums-back.

Chapter 3: two truths and a lie about the mental load

1. Douglas Cook, "Stay-at-Home Moms Work on Average 2.5 Full-time Jobs," Mass Live, January 20, 2020, https://www.masslive .com/news/2020/01/stay-at-home-moms-work-on-average-25-full -time-jobs.html.

Chapter 4: the weight of it all

1. Warren Farrell and John Gray, *The Boy Crisis: Why Our Boys Are Struggling and What We Can Do About It* (BenBella Books, 2018).
2. Louann Brizendine, *The Female Brain* (Penguin Random House, 2006), 5.
3. Matt Puderbaugh and Prabhu D. Emmady, "Neuroplasticity," National Center for Biotechnology Information, May 1, 2023, https://www.ncbi.nlm.nih.gov/books/NBK557811/.
4. C. F. Ferris et al., "Pup Suckling Is More Rewarding Than Cocaine: Evidence from Munctional Magnetic Resonance Imaging and Three-Dimensional Computational Analysis," *Journal of Neuroscience* 25, no. 1 (2005): 149–56, https://doi.org/10.1523/jneurosci.3156-04.2005.
5. Erika Barba-Mueller et al., "Brain Plasticity in Pregnancy and the Postpartum Period: Links to Maternal Caregiving and Mental

Health," *Archives of Women's Mental Health* 22 (2018): 289–99, https://doi.org/10.1007%2Fs00737-018-0889-z.

6. Linda Rose Ennis, ed., *Intensive Mothering: The Cultural Contradictions of Modern Motherhood* (Demeter Press, 2014), https://www.jstor.org/stable/j.ctt1rrd8rb.23.

7. Christianna Silva, "The Millennial Obsession with Self-Care," *NPR*, June 4, 2017, https://www.npr.org/2017/06/04/531051473 /the-millennial-obsession-with-self-care; Caroline Beaton, "Why Millennials Are Obsessed with Self-Improvement," *Psychology Today*, May 29, 2017, https://www.psychologytoday.com/us/blog /the-gen-y-guide/201705/why-millennials-are-obsessed-with -self-improvement.

8. Pratyusha Tummala-Narra, "Contemporary Impingements on Mothering," *American Journal of Psychoanalysis* 69 (2009): 4–21, https://doi.org/10.1057/ajp.2008.37; Jean-Anne Sutherland, "Mothering, Guilt, and Shame," *Sociology Compass* 4, no. 5 (2010): 310–21, https://doi.org/10.1111/j.1751-9020.2010.00283.x.

9. Miriam Liss et al., "Development and Validation of a Quantitative Measure of Intensive Parenting Attitudes," *Journal of Child and Family Studies* 22 (2012): 621–36, https://doi .org/10.1007/s10826-012-9616-y.

10. Emily A. Harris et al., "Gender Inequalities in Household Labor Predict Lower Sexual Desire in Women Partnered with Men," *Archives of Sexual Behavior* 51, no. 8 (2022): 3847–70, https://doi .org/10.1007/s10508-022-02397-2.

11. Eva Johansen et al., "Fairer Sex: The Role of Relationship Equity in Female Sexual Desire," *Journal of Sex Research* 60, no. 4 (2023): 498–507, https://doi.org/10.1080/00224499.2022.2079111.

12. Louann Brizendine, *The Female Brain* (Penguin Random House, 2006).

Chapter 7: what does she want?

1. John Gottman and Julie Schwartz Gottman, *The Man's Guide to Women: Scientifically Proven Secrets from the Love Lab about What Women Really Want* (Rodale, 2016), 146.

2. Gottman and Gottman, *Man's Guide to Women*, 8–9.

Chapter 8: what does he want?

1. Louann Brizendine, *The Male Brain* (Penguin Random House, 2010).
2. Brizendine, *The Male Brain*, 97.
3. Edward Tronick et al., "The Infant's Response to Entrapment Between Contradictory Messages in Face-to-Face Interaction," *Journal of the American Academy of Child Psychiatry* 17, no. 1 (1978): 1–13, https://doi.org/10.1016/S0002-7138(09)62273-1.
4. Marianne Sonnby-Borgström et al., "Gender Differences In Facial Imitation and Verbally Reported Emotional Contagion From Spontaneous to Emotionally Regulated Processing Levels," *Scandinavian Journal of Psychology* 49, no. 2 (2008): 111–22, https://doi.org/10.1111/j.1467-9450.2008.00626.x.
5. Avrum G. Weiss, *Hidden in Plain Sight: How Men's Fears of Women Shape Their Intimate Relationships* (Connection Victory Publishing, 2021).
6. Weiss, *Hidden in Plain Sight*.
7. Laurie J. Watson, "6 Truths About Men and Sex," *Psychology Today*, August 12, 2017, https://www.psychologytoday.com/us/blog/married-and-still-doing-it/201708/6-truths-about-men-and-sex.

Chapter 9: where do they come from?

1. Stacy Jo Dixon, "Social Media—Statistics and Facts," *Statista*, July 16, 2024, https://www.statista.com/topics/1164/social-networks/.

Chapter 14: avoiding behaviors that backfire

1. "The Buffett Formula: Going to Bed Smarter Than When You Woke Up," *Farnam Street* (blog), accessed August 22, 2024, https://fs.blog/the-buffett-formula/.

Chapter 17: for the mental load

1. Eve Rodsky, *Fair Play: A Game-Changing Solution for When You Have Too Much to Do (and More Life to Live)* (Penguin Random House, 2019), 256–60.

Chapter 20: a plan for a great sex life

1. "Modern Marriage," Pew Research Center, July 18, 2007, https://www.pewresearch.org/social-trends/2007/07/18/modern-marriage/.
2. Erick Janssen and John Bancroft, "The Dual Control Model of Sexual Response: A Scoping Review, 2009–2022," *The Journal of Sex Research* 60, no. 7 (2023): 948–68, https://doi.org/10.1080/00224499.2023.2219247.
3. Emily Nagoski, *Come As You Are: The Surprising New Science That Will Transform Your Sex Life* (Scribe, 2015).
4. Nagoski, *Come As You Are.*
5. Michael J. Rosenfeld, "Who Wants the Breakup? Gender and Breakup in Hetersexual Couples," in *Frontiers in Sociology and Social Research*, ed. Duane F. Alwin et al., vol. 2, *Social Networks and the Life Course: Integrating the Development of Human Lives and Social Relational Networks* (Springer, 2018), 221–43.